THE
TRANSFORMATIONAL
CIO

THE
TRANSFORMATIONAL
CIO

Leadership and Innovation
Strategies for IT Executives
in a Rapidly Changing World

HUNTER MULLER

WILEY

John Wiley & Sons, Inc.

Published by John Wiley & Sons, Inc., Hoboken, New Jersey.
Published simultaneously in Canada.

For general information on our other products and services or for technical support,
please contact our Customer Care Department within the United States at (800) 762-2974,
outside the United States at (317) 572-3993, or via fax at (317) 572-4002.

Wiley also publishes its books in a variety of electronic formats. Some content that
appears in print may not be available in electronic books. For more information
about Wiley products, visit our web site at www.wiley.com.

Library of Congress Cataloging-in-Publication Data:
Muller, Hunter.
   The transformational CIO: leadership and innovation strategies for IT executives in
a rapidly changing world/Hunter Muller.
      p. cm.
   Includes index.
   ISBN 978-0-470-64755-4 (cloth); ISBN 978-1-118-01932-0 (ebk);
   ISBN 978-1-118-01978-8 (ebk); ISBN 978-1-118-01979-5 (ebk)
   1.   Information technology—Management—Case studies. 2.   Chief information
officers—Case studies. I. Title.
   HD30.2.M875 2011
   004.068'4—dc22

                                                              2010045216

Printed in the United States of America

10 9 8 7 6 5 4 3

For Sandra, Chase, and Brice

CONTENTS

PREFACE

The Indispensable Executive

None of the essential transformative processes can be achieved or sustained without information technology. As a result, the chief information officer, more commonly known as the CIO, will play a central and indispensable role as a leader and enabler of business transformation. The CIO's new role is vastly different from the roles played by the previous generation of CIOs.

Unlike the CIOs of the recent decade, the modern CIO must take an active hand in developing and guiding the multiple processes required to achieve the company's strategic goals. This represents a sharp break with the past, when the primary responsibility of IT was serving internal customers and responding to the expressed needs of business units operating within the traditional boundaries of the enterprise.

The modern CIO works in the cloud, both figuratively and literally. There are no boundaries—just an infinite set of potential futures, waiting to be brought into existence.

In this truly quantum universe, the CIO's portfolio of responsibilities includes hundreds of duties. Some of these duties are abstract, some are concrete; some are obvious, some are subtle. Some require patience and humility; some require risk-taking and hubris.

Over the next 200 pages, we will look at the role of the transformational CIO and see how it is actually very similar to the roles played by other senior corporate executives. We will assemble a portrait of the "modern CIO" through stories, anecdotes, case studies, and topical research.

All of the sources interviewed for this book will provide actionable guidance, based on their own personal experiences and accumulated wisdom. You are free to follow their counsel or chart a path of your own. I promise that you will learn something useful from the stories they tell, and that you will come away with a stronger understanding of transformational IT leadership when you have read the book.

What You Will Find in This Book

Ideally, this book will serve as a helpful and very general guide for CIOs, IT leaders, and IT suppliers. It is by no means exhaustive, but it does cover many of the critical topics that concern IT executives struggling to manage successfully in today's rapidly changing markets.

The book's opening chapters are arranged loosely around a four-step process model. The subsequent chapters deal with crucial matters, such as partnering with the business, how to think like a CEO, what to do in your first 30 days on the job, and how to prepare for the next steps on your career path.

I have included as many charts and graphs as possible to help you visualize the main points of my argument. I have also included numerous examples of real-world situations in which IT leaders successfully managed the types of challenges and issues that, sooner or later, you are likely to confront in your career. I sincerely hope that you find these examples both interesting and useful.

Methodology

Before plunging onward, a few brief words on methodology are appropriate. I have been actively involved as a consultant in this field for more than 20 years. Much of what I'm writing is based on my own personal observations of top executives at leading organizations operating in major markets all over the world.

For the purpose of this book, I assembled an experienced editorial team that interviewed dozens of respected IT executives and industry experts, and crafted these interviews into stories and anecdotes revealing the multitude of challenges and opportunities facing transformational leaders in various sectors of the global economy.

Additionally, we combed through hundreds of books and thousands of articles, searching for clues that would lead us to a better understanding of how transformational strategy plays out in the real world.

I also leveraged the capabilities and resources of my firm, HMG Strategy LLC, to conduct surveys, analyze data, and generate information that will likely prove useful to anyone who is involved in a transformation project. The results of these surveys are interspersed throughout the book, and will also be available on my web site, www .hmgstrategy.com.

ACKNOWLEDGMENTS

Although this book is based primarily on the knowledge and experience that I acquired over nearly three decades as a consultant in the IT industry, the book is also a work of journalism and reportage, and I could not have completed it without leveraging the collective wisdom of many knowledgeable sources. To them I am deeply indebted. I thank them sincerely for their time, their energy, their intelligence, and their support.

I am especially grateful to Rich Adduci, Yuri Aguiar, Saad Ayub, Shawn Banerji, Roger Berry, Laxman K. Badiga, Ramón Baez, Eric Belove, Marc Benioff, Mitch Bishop, Larry Bonfante, Greg Buoncontri, Lee Congdon, Jay Crotts, Stephen Davy, John Dietrich, José Carlos Eiras, Dan Fallon, Philip Fasano, Greg Fell, Rich Gius, Stephen Gold, Katie Graham, Mark Griesbaum, Tarun Inuganti, Sheila Jordan, Emmet B. Keeffe III, Steven Kendrick, Winnie Ko, Harvey Koeppel, Roberta Kowalishin, Frank Kovacs, Robin Johnson, Andy Lark, Tony Leng, Beverly Lieberman, Peter Logothetis, Brian Lurie, Bryan MacDonald, Mark P. McDonald, Stuart McGuigan, Diana Melick, Rajeev Mehta, Tim O'Malley, Keri Pearlson, Mike Pellegrino, John Phillips, Mark Polansky, Joseph A. Puglisi, Perry Rotella, Howard Rubin, James Satterthwaite, Stephen Savage, Kara Schiltz, Phil Schneidermeyer, Tony Scott, David

Smoley, David Somers, Patrick Toole, Pamela Warren, Robert Webb, and Hank Zupnick.

Additionally, I am grateful for the assistance and support of my colleagues at HMG Strategy, Melissa Marr and Michaela Cerrone.

I also extend my sincere thanks to Sheck Cho and Stacey Rivera, my editors at John Wiley & Sons, who had faith in the value of the project and were patient when I missed my deadlines.

I owe a special debt of gratitude to Mike Barlow, the co-author of *Partnering with the CIO* (John Wiley & Sons, 2007) and *The Executive's Guide to Enterprise Social Media Strategy* (John Wiley & Sons, 2011). Mike served as my editorial director for *The Transformational CIO* book project, and his guidance was truly invaluable. In addition to being a talented writer and communicator, Mike is an all-around good guy. Thank you, Mike!

Most of all, I want to thank my wife, Sandra, who put up with long nights of writing, endless phone calls, and lost weekends of heavy editing.

INTRODUCTION

The best way to predict the future is to create it.

—Peter Drucker

Don't Be Afraid to Change Your Game

In my younger days, I was a highly competitive athlete. My primary sport was slalom skiing, and I was good enough to win two state championships when I was in high school. At various times in my life I have competed in football, wrestling, baseball, tennis, golf, and sailing. I guess you can say that competitive sports have played a significant role in my life. They have shaped me into the person I am today.

As an athlete, you learn early that every competitive experience exposes you to a different set of challenges. You learn to assess the situation rapidly, figure out how it is different, and adapt to it. In other words, you are continually *changing your game*.

Your ability to change, to adjust, to transform yourself becomes your greatest competitive advantage as an athlete. A former sportswriter told me that I fit the mold of the "intrepid athlete" because no matter what the circumstances, I'll always find a way to adjust my strategy and gain the edge over the competition.

You can only push these sports analogies so far when you're talking about business, but I think this one is valid, especially if you are a chief information officer or IT leader.

If you're going to succeed in a transformational role, you must be ready to change yourself. Sometimes the change will be a matter of fine-tuning, sometimes it will require much more. Part of your job is determining how much you have to change to achieve your goal—and then making that change as completely and as thoroughly as possible.

When I interviewed Pat Toole, the CIO of IBM, I was struck by the depth and the sincerity of the company's commitment to change. Like many of his colleagues at IBM, Pat survived the company's near-death experience in the 1990s. He doesn't have to imagine the existential danger posed by standing still—he feels it in his gut.

A full century after its birth, IBM remains a compelling story of corporate success. Even though it has racked up seven straight years of double-digit earnings per share growth, IBM is still grinding through a mind-boggling process of trimming *billions of dollars* from its operating costs.

Accompanying its all-encompassing campaign to reduce costs is an equally impressive strategy to drive innovative practices into every nook and cranny of the company—which isn't easy when you consider the size and scope of IBM's worldwide operations.

Pat sits near the center of this epic transformation, and yet he seems quite calm. He knows the magnitude of the challenge, and he understands the risks. His job isn't protecting the status quo—his job is tearing it down and replacing it with something better.

Pat uses the word "restlessness" to describe the culture at IBM. When you're restless, you can't sit still. You seek change. You welcome what's new and different; you embrace the future.

I'm not sure that I would want to have Pat's job, but I certainly respect his determination. When I look at Pat, I see a transformational CIO.

What You Need to Know *Now* about Business Transformation Strategy

Business transformation is really another way of saying "business responding appropriately to changes in the market." The reason that business transformation is terribly important right now, however, is simple: In today's unpredictable economy, markets are changing very quickly—but most businesses are still changing very slowly.

Moreover, the changes rippling across the global economy are not producing uniform effects. Some markets are changing faster and more profoundly than others. It's almost as if the laws of economics were applied haphazardly, generating different results in different markets. Faced with this kind of uncertainty, many companies choose to wait it out. But this sort of approach merely guarantees an even *slower* response to changing market conditions.

For many companies, the inability to respond appropriately to sudden changes in their markets will prove fatal. I won't speculate about which companies are spiraling downward into the dustbin of history, but I'll wager you a fine dinner that they are the companies that are ill-prepared for change.

The winners, on the other hand, will be the companies that prepare for change and nurture a corporate culture that embraces continuous business transformation. These winners will develop processes and frameworks that enable and support continuous business transformation, they will reward the people who come up with the innovations that fuel and energize continuous transformation, and they will go to market first (or second) with the products and services generated through their business transformation processes.

The New Yin and Yang of IT

Innovative use of technology is a prime requisite for success in today's markets. It's not the only requisite, but it's difficult to imagine an organization succeeding without it.

From the CIO's perspective, however, it seems impossible to consider innovation without considering costs. In the CIO's mind, innovation is inextricably linked with applications development. By the common calculus of IT budgeting, resources for apps development are created by extracting fixed costs from IT operations (i.e., "keeping the lights on").

But that means the CIO always has to justify new spending by showing how much money it will save. That kind of approach made sense 18 months ago, but as the competition heats up again, it doesn't seem like a formula for growth. As an old boss used to say, you can never save your way to greatness.

I submit that a new equation needs to be written. Instead of trying to balance innovation and cost cutting, the new formula balances innovation and value creation. After all, what really matters to the business, creating value or cutting costs? You already know the answer.

For the next couple of years, at least, the role of the CIO will be to navigate a practical course away from the old paradigm, which forced every IT expense to be counterbalanced by an anticipated savings, and move toward a new paradigm in which IT investments are justified by how much value they will create.

The "old" yin-yang was innovation and cost savings; the "new" yin-yang is innovation and business value. Welcome to the latest cycle in the continually unfolding IT saga.

Personally, I believe that the severe economic challenges of the past few years have created a new breed of transformational CIOs who are highly innovative, extremely cost-conscious, *and* acutely aware of the need to create value. In today's tumultuous business environment, this dual responsibility does not seem odd—it seems normal.

Is Everyone Really a Transformational Leader?

Last year, I hosted a high-level, invitation-only conference for about 120 CIOs and senior technology executives at major companies in the Chicago area. The conference's title was "The CIO as Transformational Leader" and its general purpose was preparing CIOs for the multiple challenges of rapidly changing global markets.

Predictably, one of the keynote presenters asked the assembled executives for a show of hands to indicate how many considered themselves to be a "transformational leader."

Practically everyone in the room raised a hand. I remember thinking, "Wow, that's great. Everyone here is already a transformational leader." Then I thought, "Wait a second. If everyone in this room is already a transformational leader, what's the point of this event?"

Before I could think too deeply about this, the presenter moved on to his next slide, and my concerns were quickly forgotten—until a few days later, when I had the good fortune to be chatting on the phone with Philip Fasano, the CIO of Kaiser Permanente. When the subject turned to business transformation, Philip made a remark that brought me back to that moment in Chicago when everyone raised their hands. Here is what Philip said:

Just because you're the CIO doesn't automatically make you a transformational *CIO*.

Philip's remark really got me thinking hard about what it means to be a transformational CIO. I wondered what you had to achieve to qualify as "transformational." Most of this book is devoted to answering that question.

You will read more about Philip and his amazing accomplishments at Kaiser Permanente in the chapters that follow. You will also read about the achievements of CIOs and senior executives at IBM, Microsoft, Siemens, Dell, Shell Oil, Citigroup, Hilton, Cisco, General Motors, General Electric, Walt Disney Parks and Resorts, CVS Caremark, Kimberly-Clark, Salesforce.com, Flextronics, Boston Scientific, Pitney Bowes, Red Hat, Cognizant, Stryker, Terex, Wipro, Frontier Communications, EMCOR, Verisk Analytics, QBE the Americas, and the United States Tennis Association.

By my own estimation, all of the CIOs interviewed for this book qualify as transformational. All of them have successfully guided large-scale, company-wide projects resulting in significant changes to the operating processes of their companies. In many instances, these transformational projects also set the stage for deep and fundamental shifts in company strategy.

I have also included interviews with some of the leading lights of the executive search industry, because their unique behind-the-scenes perspectives are genuinely valuable to anyone who has built—or is building—a career in this industry. I am fortunate to know many executive recruiters, and the presence of these experts in the book imparts a certain *gravitas* that might be otherwise lacking.

Chapter 5, "Mapping *Your* Future," is structured around the comments and insight of industry experts at Korn/Ferry International, Egon Zehnder International, Russell Reynolds Associates, Spencer Stuart, Heidrick & Struggles, Halbrecht Lieberman Associates, and Hodge Partners.

Assembling an "all-star" cast of experienced IT leaders and business experts wasn't easy, and I am grateful to all of them for taking the time to speak with me and to work closely with my editorial team. I am certain that you will find their collective wisdom to be valuable and helpful.

As you have probably already discovered, there really is no manual or field guide detailing the process of becoming a transformational CIO. This book is more of a manifesto, which is, according to the Merriam-Webster online dictionary, "a written statement declaring publicly the intentions, motives, or views of its issuer." The definition in my dog-eared copy of *The Random House Dictionary of the English Language* is similar, but seems to strike a little closer to the bone: "A public declaration of intentions, opinions, objectives or motives . . . "

So there you have it. Call this book a manifesto—a collection of intentions and opinions, carefully gathered from top practitioners in the field, and presented here for your consideration.

Moving Target

Early in the writing of this book, I noticed that almost everyone I spoke with seemed to have developed their own personal interpretation of the word "transformational."

Some applied the word loosely to cover any change initiative that was reasonably complex. Some were quite strict in their use of the word, reserving it to describe large-scale projects affecting broad constituencies inside and outside the enterprise.

Still others used it to describe improvements or innovations that permanently altered an organization's bedrock culture.

Everyone, it seemed, agreed that the introduction of new technology by itself rarely qualifies as "transformational"—unless it results in sweeping changes across multiple areas of an organization.

I mention these disparities to highlight the dangers of trying too hard to define something that is essentially an abstract concept. Words such as "transformation" and "transformational" are moving targets. Their perceived meanings change and evolve over time. So please don't be surprised if you notice that no two individuals quoted in this book use the words "transformation" or "transformational" in exactly the same way. This is one instance in which the dictionary offers us little practical help.

As Albert Einstein observed, it all depends on your frame of reference.

Transformation, Then and Now

Back in the spring of 1995, *Harvard Business Review* published an article by John Kotter, then a professor of leadership at Harvard Business School in Boston. The title of the article was "Leading Change." The subtitle was "Why Transformation Efforts Fail."

The article previewed a book of the same title that was published the following year. I think it's entirely fair to say that Kotter's writing defined the way that most of us understand the concept of business transformation.

If you are familiar with the book, you will remember that Kotter describes an eight-stage approach for moving ahead successfully with transformation projects. Kotter's revolutionary process now seems like common sense, which demonstrates the extent to which we have internalized his original insights.

Given the hypermercurial quality of today's global economy, however, I believe that a faster and more flexible method is required. I have developed a four-step model that distills the critical stages of earlier models, reduces complexity, and eliminates steps that now seem redundant.

The model is designed to make it easier for CIOs to succeed in their roles as transformational leaders. The model provides a simple, practical framework for developing transformation projects, rolling them out smoothly, and making them operational within the accelerated timeframes that now seem quite natural to us.

Four Steps to Success

The model's four steps are *define, build, lead,* and *change.*

1. *Define.* The first step is defining the vision that will guide the transformation project from beginning to end. Each of the four steps in the model is critical, but it is absolutely imperative that you get this one right for the simple reason that you won't be able to succeed unless a critical mass of people can visualize the end result that you are driving to achieve. In other words, the people who carry out the transformation project must have a clear view of its objective and they must share a common understanding of why the project is important.

2. *Build.* The second step is building the executive team that will convert the vision into reality and deliver the expected results, on time and on budget. As the CIO, you must build an executive team that reflects your passion and your commitment to change.

That probably means that you will have to rearrange your organization, bring in some new players, and move some people into different roles. Some of this will be difficult, but it is work that you need to do, because you will be relying on your executive team to accomplish the heavy lifting required to complete the project successfully.

3. *Lead.* The third step is creating a culture of leadership that inspires trust and confidence within the IT organization and across the enterprise. This step represents a sharp break with past practice, in which the IT organization functioned in a largely reactive mode, typically responding to the needs of the business. This step fundamentally alters the relationship between IT and the enterprise. In a very real sense, it's a game changer. When you tackle this step, you're sending a new message to the business that says, "IT is your equal. We will continue helping you, but we will also advise you and guide you so you can leverage the full power of modern information technology."

4. *Change.* The fourth step is actually changing the way people think and behave, not just while the transformation project is taking place, but over the long term. This step makes the transformation complete, because it marries the three essentials—people, process, and technology—and lays down a solid foundation for the next inevitable round of transformational activity. After you have accomplished this step, you can take a brief moment to rest on your laurels and congratulate yourself for a job well done.

Since each of the model's four steps represents a distillation of many substeps, the model serves as an overarching framework rather than as a tactical plan.

That being said, the steps should be addressed in their numerical order. With the obvious exception of Step 1, each subsequent step builds on the previous step. As a consequence, every step is essential, and none of the four steps can be safely skipped or ignored. It's a little bit like flying a high performance jet fighter. You don't *have* to follow the checklist . . . but it's highly recommended that you do!

Most of the transformation projects described in this book track closely to the four steps in the model. Consciously or unconsciously, successful transformational initiatives seem to follow similar paths through the wilderness.

Great Things Happen to Great CIOs

This introduction is intended to set the stage for the chapters that follow. Before we dive into the deep end of the pool, however, I wanted to offer two brief examples of CIOs who really understand the value of building great relationships with the business.

Dave Smoley is the CIO at Flextronics, a leading electronics manufacturing services provider. Based in Singapore and operating in 30 countries, Flextronics is a large, complex enterprise—exactly the kind of organization that might find it difficult to stop on a dime and reverse course at a moment's notice. But that's just what Dave asked it to do a few months ago—and the speedy change of direction resulted in huge cost savings and greater efficiencies.

Here's what happened: The company had planned to implement a new HR system using an expensive software package from an established vendor. Financing for the new system was in place and it looked like a done deal—until Dave's IT team discovered an alternative software-as-a-service (SaaS) solution that would cost far less and impose far fewer burdens on the IT department. I'll let Dave tell the rest of the story in his own words.

We had been heading down a traditional path, people were feeling pretty good about it and this disruptive technology pops up at the last minute. I had a relationship with the CEO, the CFO, the head of HR . . . and I said to them, "Okay guys, I know we've been working on going down path A, but I want you to know this disruptive technology's popped up and I think it will be a better solution for less money. So we may switch here in the next month, depending on what we find out." And they agreed that we should check it out.

Then we spent the next couple of months testing the functionality, testing the financial model, checking the viability of the company, checking the technology stack, which is different from anything that we've been using. The partnering on this went pretty deep. We had people from IT, people from HR, people from finance, all working together. And when we were done testing, we came back and made the recommendation. We said, "There's some risk here, but it's manageable and the potential payback is huge, so let's go with it."

Our internal partnerships enabled us to act with speed and agility and evaluate a calculated risk in a very short period of time to make a decision . . . at another big company, it might not have happened . . . or it might have been hugely disruptive.

An Overhead Smash

Here's another quick story from another part of the IT universe. My good friend Larry Bonfante has been the CIO of the United States Tennis Association (USTA) for the past eight years. In addition to providing an array of services for nearly three-quarters of a million tennis players and their families, the USTA runs the U.S. Open, which is held over a two-week period in August and draws the largest crowds of any annual sporting event in the world.

If you want to get Larry going, ask him how he feels about aligning IT with the business.

To me the only objectives we have in IT are the objectives of the USTA. One thing that drives me crazy is when people in the industry talk about alignment between IT and the business— as if they're separate entities!

In my mind, there's only one business and that's the business of USTA. IT's a critical part of that business, but we're not aligned with the business because we're a part of the business. What drives us is the mission of the association. Whatever the objectives of my business colleagues are, those are our objectives. We're here to provide solutions and services that will enable the USTA to meet its objectives.

As you can see, Larry is the kind of CIO who gets along nicely with the business. For Larry, the relationship between

IT and the larger organization is truly a partnership. The result of this partnership has been some impressive wins—for IT and the business.

For example, when Larry asked for additional funding to provide wireless services for vendors on the edges of the USTA's 10-acre campus in Flushing Meadows, the request wasn't presented as an IT project. It was presented as a business project with an IT component. The issue, as Larry explains, was that the vendor kiosks at the periphery of the campus were not tethered into the site's sales systems. As a consequence, those vendors could accept only cash.

Like any responsible business, the USTA resists requests for unbudgeted spending. But thanks to Larry's rapport with the organization's executive leadership, the request for additional funding was approved.

The results were better than an overhead smash: The wireless network enabled the kiosks to accept credit and debit cards, which sent sales skyrocketing. The $50,000 investment in new technology rapidly generated $150,000 in additional sales—a 300 percent return on investment!

And as a bonus, guests, players, and journalists at the U.S. Open now had access to a wireless network!

A Model for Transformation

Robert Webb is the CIO at Hilton Worldwide, the globally respected hospitality company. Hilton Worldwide spans more than 3,600 hotels and 600,000 rooms in 82 countries. The company includes famous brands such as Waldorf Astoria Hotels & Resorts, Conrad Hotels & Resorts, Hilton Hotels & Resorts, Doubletree, Embassy Suites Hotels, Hilton Garden Inn, Hampton Hotels, Homewood Suites by Hilton, Home2 Suites by Hilton, and Hilton Grand Vacations. The company also manages the world-class guest reward program Hilton HHonors®.

Staying ahead in a continually evolving global economy requires continual transformation. One of Rob's key responsibilities is guiding a major business integration project that is transforming the company and creating competitive advantages that will serve Hilton for decades into the future. It's a huge responsibility, but I know that Rob can handle the job. I'll let him tell the story in his own words:

> *We're a very large company, with a full spectrum of hotels and properties across the globe. We have grown significantly over the years, including through the merger of brands and the reuniting of Hilton Hotels Corporation and Hilton International, which had operated separately for more than four decades.*
>
> *Now we are integrating all the various parts of the company so we can act as one global unified business. We've moved our corporate headquarters from Beverly Hills to McLean, Virginia, and we've undertaken a technology-enabled transformation. At the heart of this transformation is something we call the Hilton Innovation Collaborative, which is a strategic sourcing program that partners Hilton with some of the world's best-in-class organizations.*
>
> *In the first year that I was here, we completed transformational sourcing deals with IBM, Microsoft, Accenture, AT&T*

and Tata. For example, we transitioned our data center in Memphis to IBM, and we moved our domestic and Canadian high-speed Internet access program to AT&T. . . . We've asked all of the suppliers participating in the Innovation Collaborative to invest in helping us build our next generation of technology.

These agreements, combined with resources in a dedicated investment fund, create a snowball effect that enables Rob's team to keep the transformational strategy moving along at a quick tempo.

We're accelerating the implementation of new financial systems, new collaboration systems, new infrastructure, and a whole host of new applications such as revenue management and property management, which are strategic differentiators for us.

It's been a massive change from a people perspective. When everything was managed within Hilton, we had about 1,600 people in IT. Now we're moving to a model where about 500 of those people will be Hilton employees and about 1,500 people will be working with us through our partners. So we'll have more people in total, but the delivery model will be vastly different than what it was before. This is a 180-degree shift in our technology strategy.

A CIO needs vision, energy and discipline to lead a transformation of this scale and complexity. Rob has all three. Here is his take on how the role of the CIO has evolved to keep pace with the changing global markets:

When I began my executive responsibilities several years ago, we weren't as reliant on outside providers as we are now. Today it makes absolute sense to tap into the capabilities of your suppliers in a much deeper way than before. As a consequence, the CIO has to manage SLAs [service level agreements], set program roadmaps, handle complicated contractual negotiations, and create governance mechanisms among multiple suppliers. The CIO needs a different mix of skills than in the past. Today's CIO needs business leadership skills, in addition to core technology skills, to successfully manage all of the relationships. Of course, you cannot transition the responsibility for getting things right. You have to provide leadership and you have to make sure that your suppliers stay focused on the customer.

From Rob's perspective, the modern CIO is part business integrator, part relationship manager, part innovator and part strategy leader. When you put all those parts together, you get a model for effective transformation.

Chapter 1

Vision and Organization

Executive Summary

Defining the vision is the essential first step in any successful transformation plan. As CIO, you should be able to describe the vision and convey its critical importance to the organization in as few words as possible. The next key step is building or restructuring an effective IT leadership team that will support your transformational efforts—and watch your back.

Bringing the Vision to Life

In this chapter, we look primarily at three successful transformation scenarios to get a better idea of why it's critical to define a vision—clearly and unambiguously—before moving forward. After defining the vision, the next logical step is building the leadership team you'll need to turn the vision into reality.

One of the key takeaways from this chapter is that the transformational vision doesn't have to be overly complex or wildly ambitious—in fact, it helps if the vision is simple, straightforward, and easy to describe in a couple of short sentences.

And the vision doesn't have to emerge full-blown from the mind of the CIO. What counts is that the vision is tethered firmly to a business objective—or to an "end state"—that can be described in terms that everyone understands.

For a decade, Roger Berry served as senior vice president and chief information officer at Walt Disney Parks and Resorts, a division of the Walt Disney Company. The division operates nine theme parks, a cruise line business, and more than 30 major resorts and hotels in locations around the world.

Roger played a key leadership role in the division's transformation from a very effective but traditionally focused hospitality business into a truly guest-centric organization. He credits Allen "Al" Weiss, the executive who brought him to Disney, with the original vision that guided the transformation.

The vision of a guest-centric organization was initially expressed in 2000 by Al, who was president of Walt Disney World at that time. I'll let Roger tell the story in his own words:

> *Al had a vision of transforming the focus of the Disney theme park experience to ensure the brand was in step and aligned with the emerging personalized service trend. At that time, we offered what was pretty much a "one size fits all" experience. Al wanted to change that, but he knew instinctively that he couldn't transform and deliver the vision without the right technology strategy in place.*

The key to making it work technically was creating an incredibly tight alignment of all the various guest-focused core business processes and IT systems. The electronic integration would allow Disney to engage and personalize the guest experience from the first call to the customer contact center to the bus ride back to the airport. It was a tall order, but with great people and strong executive support, Roger's team got it done.

As suggested in the book's introduction, the real hurdles weren't posed by the technology. The hardest obstacles to overcome were cultural. As in many companies, the division had grown accustomed to the traditional role of IT as a back-office function. A big part of Roger's job was changing the way people looked at IT.

> *I determined very quickly that most of the people in the business didn't understand the scale, diversity, and complexity of the technology that was in place at Disney World or what it takes to manage it. More importantly they didn't realize what it would take from the business to achieve the level of integration required to realize the vision. Consequently, IT was taken for granted by some and naturally, the staff in IT felt as though they were underappreciated.*
>
> *We were doing some good things in IT, but we were performing in the traditional mode. The key business areas set the strategy and decided what it needed, came up with a proposed solution and handed it to IT to execute. In some situations they would even pursue the execution themselves.*
>
> *In that model, IT had little strategic influence on the direction of the business and was sometimes handed an almost impossible situation to deliver. Consequently, the view of IT's strategic value was underestimated. If the systems came up on time in the morning and the key reports were out . . . IT was doing a good job. . . .*

Roger knew that he had to correct these misperceptions if IT had any chance of enabling the vision.

"The first thing we had to do was help the business understand the role of IT in enabling this transformation," says Roger. "Then the next thing was making sure the IT organization understood the essential role they would play in the future of the business, and that the business was counting on them."

> ## Lesson
>
> The vision doesn't have to emerge full-blown from the mind of the CIO. What counts is that the vision is tethered firmly to a business objective—or to an "end state"—that can be described in terms that everyone understands.

Roger started out by explaining how the trend toward digital and process convergence, which was still a relatively new concept at the time, was opening opportunities for technology to advance process speed and efficiency across the business. Further, it required IT influence to expand beyond the "back office" and out onto the front lines of guest service. In other words, IT had to be a key player in the strategy and how it was to be designed and implemented.

Roger also knew that he would need an emotional appeal to "win the hearts and minds" of the 600 people working in the division's IT organization.

In a brainstorming session with his IT executive team focused on cast communication, a slide was put up of Mickey Mouse holding the hand of a small child walking blissfully down Main Street at the Magic Kingdom.

I pointed to the slide and said, "That connection between Mickey and a child is the essence of our business. That is the magic and the magical memory the child and the family will carry with them forever, in their minds, their hearts and in their photo albums. . . . "

Finally, after a couple of hours of brainstorming, one member of the IT team said, "We may not make the magic but we play an essential role in making that magical connection happen!" That was the emotional connection we were searching for!

We then came up with the tagline for IT: "We don't make the magic . . . we make Magical Connections." *We then revised it to* "IT . . . Making Magical Connections."

Roger and his executive team then set out to build a brand identity for IT. They designed an IT logo depicting an image of the world adorned with Mickey's distinctive ears. The design is set against Mickey's official colors—red, black, and yellow—and appears to be breaking out of the background. The purpose of the design was to emphasize the relationship between IT and the core business, and to show that IT was thinking "outside the box" to deliver innovative services.

The IT logo was eventually printed on signs, placards, and T-shirts. Being part of Disney, they even put the logo on a pin, which is now considered a collector's item. These items were then awarded to the IT cast for recognition of a job well done and to continually reinforce the critical role they play in the business . . . every day!

The new logo was officially introduced at a "brand launch" for IT. The event was held in the largest ballroom at Disney's ultra-modern Contemporary Resort near the Magic Kingdom in Orlando. Roger recalls the moment when the new logo was unveiled:

The impact was powerful and immediate. I have to tell you, it was instant alignment. When people saw it, they made the

Lesson

Find simple images or simple phrases that will help you generate the emotional tidal waves you will need to overcome the natural tendency of people to stick with the status quo.

connection and they understood the new role of IT. And they understood why we were focusing on methodology, best practices, and standards. Everything began falling into place because of that single step.

There's a great lesson here. When you're trying to get the ball rolling, be imaginative. Be positive, be happy, and be courageous. Find simple images or simple phrases that will help you generate the emotional tidal waves you will need to overcome the natural tendency of people to stick with the status quo.

For the IT organization at Disney, the IT logo was like Dumbo's magic feather—it helped them clear a cultural hurdle so they could move ahead with the real work that lay ahead.

One Transformation Leads to Another

The transformation strategy launched by Roger and his team back in 2000 moved ahead steadily for more than 10 years. Each time the IT organization launched a new technology or achieved a tighter integration with the business, a new opportunity for improving the guest experience surfaced.

"Once we had established the emotional connection between the guest experience and IT, we spun it out from there," says Roger. "We realized there were lots of magical moments involving IT, everything from booking a room over the Internet to scheduling a meal with Cinderella. So we kept at it. One of the things I love about Disney is that we won't quit on a great idea, even if it takes years to make it work."

I think that one of the best examples of how a transformational strategy can deliver a continuous stream of tangible business benefits can be seen in Disney's Magical Express Service, which is a free service that provides transportation for guests—and their luggage—from Orlando International Airport to the various Disney-managed resorts at Walt Disney World. Maybe it doesn't sound like a big deal, but here's what makes it really cool: When you get off your airplane, you go right to an air-conditioned coach bus that brings you to your resort. You don't have to worry about your luggage, because it's taken off the plane and delivered right to your hotel room.

If you've ever traveled anywhere with young kids, you can imagine how great it is to walk into your hotel room and find your luggage already there waiting for you!

And if you're an IT person, you can also imagine just how difficult it can be to integrate and manage all the internal and external IT-dependent processes required to get the guests and their luggage to their proper destinations.

Here's the best part: When you leave the resort, all of these processes run in reverse. Your luggage is whisked to the airport and placed on your airplane. You don't have to lift it, drag it, or worry about it until you get to your home airport. Now that's my kind of magic, and clearly a "magical connection!"

Needless to say, it could not be accomplished without an extremely close alignment of IT and all the various guest services required for transporting thousands of people and their possessions across miles of Florida landscape. *Making Magical Connections* is a terrific example of how an IT team with great leadership delivers on its promise to the business *and* to the business's customers.

Going Global

Ramón Baez is the vice president of Information Technology Services and chief information officer at Kimberly-Clark Corporation, the home to some of the world's most trusted and recognized brands including Kleenex®, Scott®, HUGGIES®, Pull-Ups®, Depend®, and Kotex®. Headquartered in Dallas, with nearly 56,000 employees worldwide and operations in 35 countries, Kimberly-Clark posts sales of nearly $20 billion annually. The company's brands are sold in more than 150 countries, making it a truly global enterprise.

When Ramón joined the company in 2007, he knew that one of his first tasks would be preparing the IT organization for the excruciating demands and evolving complexities of the global economy.

> " . . . you can't just talk about the organization—you have to explain to people how this vision will affect them and why it's important for them to be a part of it. Because everyone is wondering, 'what's in it for me?' That's just human nature."

As it turned out, preparing the organization for its global responsibilities took on the dimensions of a transformational project. Ramón quickly realized that he had two immediate challenges to confront.

The first challenge was putting an effective IT leadership team in place. Here's the way Ramón saw things:

We needed to do things that we had never done before in areas such as business analytics, cloud computing, outsourcing, collaboration, you name it. So we needed a real leadership team that could motivate the rest of the IT organization. It couldn't just be me—there was far too much that we needed to get done in a brief period of time.

The second challenge was convincing the business units that the IT organization would function as a trusted and indispensable strategic partner, through thick and thin.

When I arrived, I saw that a big chunk of IT had been outsourced. That was a sure indication that the company did not see IT as a strategic partner. It told me that we needed to win back the trust and the confidence of the business leaders.

It turned out that Ramón's instincts enabled him to guide the IT organization in exactly the right direction. The following years, 2008 and 2009, were disastrous for most companies. Kimberly-Clark was one of the few exceptions. Thanks in part to the groundwork laid by Ramón and his team, the company had its best year in 2009, posting $19.1 billion in global sales.

Let's take a closer look at how Ramón was able to begin transforming the IT organization and how he kept the transformational processes on track.

It started with the vision. "When you're up in front of an organization, you need a clear view of where you want to go and you must be able to explain it to people very clearly," says Ramón. "And you can't just talk about the organization—you have to explain to people how this vision will affect them and why it's important for them to be a part of it. Because everyone is wondering, 'what's in it for me?' That's just human nature."

Ramón's vision was an IT organization that partners closely with the business units to generate more sales and greater profits for the company. "More growth translates into a better future for the people in IT and for their families," says Ramón. "As a leader, you have to convey the idea of a brighter future. That doesn't mean you should be overly optimistic, but you must be positive. You have to get people excited and inspired."

He also had to address the issue of how the IT organization was perceived by the rest of the company.

Gartner and Forrester said we were great. The big vendors said we were a model shop. We got a lot of accolades, and we deserved them.

I remember sitting with 14 or 15 of our top IT leaders in a meeting back in 2007. Some of them asked me why the business didn't appreciate IT.

I told them that the company's business leaders didn't view us as value creators. And that was the reason why so much of our work had been outsourced.

Well, it was pretty devastating for them to hear that. It was a tough moment. But we had to get through the denial phase and learn to accept reality. It took us a couple of months, to be perfectly honest. Some people told me it was like a catharsis. Someone who had been with the company 25 years told me that it was a life-changing experience.

But it made everyone think about how we really needed to become a leadership team—not just for the sake of the IT organization, but for the whole company.

Building the Leadership Team

Ramón knew that one of his top priorities was building the executive team that would lead the transformation. But the process wasn't easy or quick.

First you really have to think hard about what you're planning to accomplish over the next three or four years. Then you read through the background files of the people already on the team. Then you sit down and meet with them individually. Some people will come across as very confident and very capable. Usually, those are the people you want to keep. With others, you can tell they've reached their level of incompetence—remember the Peter Principle? Those are the people you don't want to bring with you into the battle.

It's harder to decide about the people who fall in the middle. Those are the people you have to spend the most amount of time thinking about. Do they have the right strengths to help you? Will their weaknesses impede your efforts? Can they be coached? Can they improve?

In some instances, Ramón had to look outside the organization for the right person. For example, the IT organization already had an excellent infrastructure team. "They were probably the best I'd ever seen. I was very, very impressed," he recalls. "But they didn't have any experience outside the company. While there was nothing *wrong* with that, I knew that we needed someone with global experience because we were a global organization."

But the right person also had to be a deeply experienced leader who would command the respect of the infrastructure team and serve as a mentor.

"I wanted someone who would help the people on the team move up to the next level, someone who would teach them the skills they needed to become mature leaders," says Ramón. "So I waited. And I waited. People started getting angry with me and told me I should just pick someone. I started to get frustrated, and I came close to settling. But eventually I got the resume I had been looking for. It took me eight months to find exactly the right person, but it was worth it."

But having a leadership team *in place* doesn't automatically translate into success. You also need to train and develop the people that you've chosen to serve as the leaders of the organization.

"After we had our leaders in place, we helped them improve their leadership skills," explains Ramón. "We coached them to become better communicators. We taught them how to interact more effectively with all the different personalities you find in a big corporation. We prepared them for their roles as inspirational leaders. We did a lot of role playing— which was both useful and enjoyable!"

Lesson

Having a leadership team *in place* doesn't automatically translate into success. You also need to train and develop the people that you've chosen to serve as the leaders of the organization.

In addition to acquiring some new players, Ramón also restructured the leadership team. When he joined the company, he had 15 direct reports. "I had so many direct reports that I couldn't make enough time for all of them. As a result, they weren't getting the attention from me that they needed," he recalls.

He eventually reduced his direct reports to a more manageable size. "Now I have seven direct reports. Five are what we call 'delivery engines' and two are responsible for the business relationships," says Ramón.

Here's a simplified version of his org chart:

Simplified Org Chart

CIO	
	IT Infrastructure
	IT Applications Solutions
	Enterprise Business Intelligence
	Program Management
	Strategy, Technology, and Architecture
	IT Business Partner (consumer products, finance, innovation, and marketing)
	IT Business Partner (K-C International, K-C Health Care, K-C Professional, Human Resources, and Legal)

Obviously, there are many different ways in which you can structure an executive leadership team. In *The Practical CIO,* José Carlos Eiras recommends creating an "IT Board" that serves as the CIO's cabinet or inner circle of advisors. Eiras relied on this type of executive team structure to help him guide major transformational projects while he was the global CIO at General Motors Europe (see the following chart).

The IT Board

IT	Business IT	IT Support
Operations	Sales and Marketing	Finance
Planning, Strategy, PMO, Contracts	Engineering (Product Development)	Purchasing
Architecture and Standards (Application and Infrastructure)	Manufacturing	Legal
	Logistics (Supply Chain)	
	Finance and Human Resources	HR

Demonstrating Value

Rebuilding and restructuring his leadership team sent an important message to the rest of the IT organization—and to the business leaders in the company. At Kimberly-Clark, however, Ramón knew that he had to do more to change the company's general perception of IT.

> *In the old days, IT would just send someone to work in a business unit and the business leader would have no say in choosing that person. We decided that before placing IT people in the business units, we would ask the business leaders to participate in the selection process. That way, the businesses would have skin in the game and they would know that we were serious about creating value for them.*

I remember the first time that I sent e-mails to the business presidents and I said, "I have some folks lined up for you to interview." I got e-mails back from the presidents—they couldn't believe it! They said, "You want us to be part of the selection process?" And I said, "Yes, that's how it's supposed to work. That's how we operate." The business presidents were amazed. They found it very refreshing. It was a big step forward for the IT organization.

Ramón also knew that it was critical to re-establish the credibility of IT as a trusted business partner. "We needed to demonstrate that we could execute on projects on schedule, on time, and on quality," says Ramón. "That last part, 'on quality,' was the most important."

In other words, being a true partner wasn't just a matter of sticking to budgets and meeting deadlines. "The new questions we started asking ourselves were, 'Did this project meet the needs of the business? Did it help the business achieve its objective? Did we deliver value to the business?' Those became the important questions."

For example, when the global economy faltered, all of the company's leaders were told to concentrate on initiatives that would generate cash. These cash generation initiatives focused on three critical areas: working capital, organizational optimization, and global sourcing. The IT organization was involved in all three areas.

"We put together a target that was aspirational, and we exceeded our target," says Ramón. "Here we are, the IT organization, and we're generating cash for the company. The

> "We decided that before placing IT people in the business units, we would ask the business leaders to participate in the selection process. That way, the businesses would have skin in the game and they would know that we were serious about creating value for them."

business presidents were saying, 'Wow, you guys are really serious.' That's when I knew people were looking at us differently and seeing us as a value creator."

After listening to Ramón tell this story, I also thought of another lesson that it can teach us: When you have an opportunity to show the world how good you are—take it! I mentioned that to Ramón, and here's what he told me:

Absolutely. You take the opportunity and you don't complain about it. Believe it or not, when they told us we had to focus on cash generation, I heard people in IT complaining. I told them, "Hey, this isn't about IT, it's about making sure the company is stronger when we get out of this economic mess." And that's just what we did—we worked on making the company stronger. By the time 2009 finally ended, it was our strongest year.

"It's *More* about the Future"

Kaiser Permanente HealthConnect® is the $4 billion electronic medical records system rolled out in 2008 by Kaiser Permanente, the nation's largest not-for-profit health plan.

The system enables Kaiser Permanente's more than 8.6 million members in nine states to access their medical records, check the results of lab tests, and send secure messages electronically to their caregivers. It enables Kaiser Permanente's network of 80,000 caregivers to keep track of patients, write prescriptions electronically, schedule appointments, and avoid some of the costly—and occasionally dangerous—medical mistakes that invariably result from relying solely on memory or paper records.

From an IT perspective, KP HealthConnect is a technological *tour de force* that has yet to be replicated anywhere else in the world. But when you're chatting with Philip Fasano, the CIO of Kaiser Permanente, you remember that behind every great transformation is a great team of executives, employees, and customers. This one is no exception.

"You can't do it in a vacuum," says Philip. "As a CIO, you have to substantially understand the key issues of the business that you are a part of. You also have to understand the industry that your business operates in. And you have to understand the larger national or global issues that can affect your business and your industry. You have to understand all of that and see the big picture before you even attempt to articulate a vision."

Once you have begun to formulate a transformational vision, you must apply a series of reality checks. "It's extremely important for you to test your perception of the vision by meeting with other executives and business leaders across the company," says Philip. "Remember, you're not just developing a vision for the IT organization—you're developing a vision for the entire enterprise."

Philip recommends working closely with the CEO, the executive leadership team, business leaders, regional leaders, and customers to develop the broad perspective required for managing a large-scale transformational project.

"Remember, you need to think beyond today and tomorrow. Focus on what you think will be happening over the next 10 to 15 years. Think about the role that IT will play in that larger vision," says Philip. "It's more about the future than about today."

The future also includes the team of executives and managers you will rely on to make it all happen. As time passes, conditions will change. Different talents and abilities will be required. So it's important to think of the team as a work in progress. "You'll need people who can knock it out of the park today, but also grow and develop as their roles change and evolve," says Philip. "The person you hire today might not be the right person five years from now. In today's world, none of these roles are static."

"You can't do it in a vacuum. As a CIO, you have to substantially understand the key issues of the business that you are a part of. You also have to understand the industry that your business operates in. And you have to understand the larger national or global issues that can affect your business and your industry. You have to understand all of that and see the big picture before you even attempt to articulate a vision."

Maintaining the Momentum

Since transformational projects tend to play out over long timeframes, you will need to inspire, invigorate, and energize the people around you. "When you're developing a vision, don't forget about the inspirational component. You'll need something that will inspire people to keep going, something they'll understand and internalize. You need to help them make it personal."

At Kaiser Permanente, part of the inspirational message is built into the company culture, which emphasizes the overarching importance of continuous innovation. "We are a little different in that it's part of our cultural DNA," Philip explains. "From our inception as a company, we have focused on technology and innovation. In many other companies, IT and the business aren't joined together in a lot of places. In our company, IT and the business are joined together right at the top of the organization and throughout all of our partnership groups and leadership groups. IT is part of the business conversation across the organization."

That makes it easier for Philip and his team to remain positively connected with the various parts of the enterprise. While that shared sense of purpose doesn't guarantee smooth sailing for every project, it certainly makes it easier to maintain the energy and momentum required to complete a series of critical business transformations.

"Our systems transformation initiative began about six years ago. About a year later, we went to full-scale implementation across the company. Over the past three years, we've actually improved and accelerated the implementation process to the point where we can manage a hospital implementation in a matter of 30 to 60 days," says Philip. "The industry standard for a full-scale hospital implementation is typically about five years. We've really tried to perfect our approach so we can implement these major changes very rapidly."

Again, Philip attributes the success of his efforts to the broader company culture.

At its core, our culture is about providing high-quality and affordable care that is preventive, smart, networked, and collaborative. If you think about what that means, we are committed to improving patient outcomes to the point where patients stay healthy and get sick less often. We want to help patients manage illnesses before they occur. That is the goal that inspires us. That is the heart and soul of our IT organization.

So with that idea at the core, we think about transformation from the perspective of leveraging clinical data and information technology to achieve the better health outcomes for our patients.

That sense of purpose is embedded in our IT organization. We've spent a lot of time developing and communicating that message throughout the IT organization and talking about how we are fully involved and responsible in so many areas of patient care.

IT is everywhere—in labs, pharmacies, hospital rooms, clinics, surgical suites—everywhere. Physicians won't perform an operation unless the information system is available. The people in IT know this, and they take responsibility for their role in delivering care to millions of patients. We are extraordinarily

> "Remember, you need to think beyond today
> and tomorrow. Focus on what you think will
> be happening over the next 10 to 15 years.
> Think about the role that IT will play in that
> larger vision. It's more about the future than
> about today."

passionate about our role in delivering care and improving medical outcomes.

Philip says that he doesn't see an end to the process of transformation at Kaiser Permanente. "The next frontier is predictive care. That's where we use the information we have to create a new wave of innovation in health care. In the past, most of the great medical discoveries came from the sciences of biology and chemistry. The next series of great discoveries will come from the science of information. We're just on the cusp of that wave now. It's very exciting and the potential benefits are enormous—healthier people *and* lower health care costs."

Don't Be Afraid to Inspire People

What I really love about these three CIOs is that none of them was afraid to step up and lead. And what thoroughly amazes me is how comfortable they became in their roles as inspirational leaders.

To me, inspirational leaders are a cut above the usual executive. They don't yell, they don't scream, they don't threaten, and they don't bully.

They project strength, resiliency, and even toughness—but they do it in a calm, confident manner that puts people at ease and inspires them to do their best work.

Somehow, inspirational leaders figure out how to lead others by being great role models. When we think of great inspirational leaders from the past, we usually think of people like George Washington, Thomas Jefferson, and Abraham Lincoln—passionate about their beliefs, cool under fire, and tough as nails. A list of inspirational leaders from recent history would certainly include Mahatma Gandhi, Martin Luther King Jr., Lech Walesa, and the Dalai Lama. Each confronted powerful challenges without losing the sense of inner peace that inspired their followers to keep fighting, no matter how daunting the odds.

Roger Berry told me a story about a conversation he had with his dad many years ago while they were fishing. At the time, Roger was considering leaving his job at Tenneco Gas and going to work for Campbell Soup. He was concerned about how he would fare in a new environment. After a bit of conversation, his dad told him to stop worrying. And he gave him some excellent advice: *Always remember that you're only as good as the people who follow you.*

I interpret his advice to mean that if you have good people following you, helping you, and supporting your efforts, you will probably succeed. Inspirational leaders intuitively grasp this simple fact of life, and they weave it tightly into their leadership style.

"When you're developing a vision, don't forget about the inspirational component. You'll need something that will inspire people to keep going, something they'll understand and internalize. You need to help them make it personal."

Chapter 2

Culture and Change

Executive Summary

If business transformations could be achieved solely through the replacement of old technology with newer technology, they wouldn't be so difficult and they wouldn't pose so many problems. Successful transformation strategies are all about people and culture. A transformation that doesn't transform behaviors widely and generally across the enterprise isn't really much of a transformation.

In this chapter, we focus on the experiences of CIOs who led transformational efforts that were designed primarily to change the culture of their organizations. In many respects, these kinds of cultural transformations are more difficult than transformations driven mostly by the need for rapid technological change. When the culture of the IT organization changes, relationships between IT and the rest of the company are altered, fundamentally and profoundly.

Overturning the Status Quo

If you ask Rich Adduci to name his favorite role throughout his career, he will tell you without hesitation that it was transforming the IT organization at Boston Scientific Corporation (BSC), one of the world's largest makers of advanced medical devices.

When Rich joined Boston Scientific as its CIO in 2006, about 80 percent of the IT professionals in the company reported to executives or managers outside of IT. Here is his recollection of the situation:

The people who performed IT services were decentralized, reporting to various functions (such as finance, operations, or human resources) or to the business units. There was really no coordination of IT activities across the company, and few IT standards or policies existed. The people themselves were in small organizations with little future career growth and often not being well recognized for the level of their contribution since they were being evaluated by non-IT managers.

He quickly determined that the status quo was unsustainable.

We were operating in a highly regulated environment; I saw several decentralized IT groups building systems that solved the exact same problem and not following a standard methodology or policy set. We had just completed a major acquisition with aging systems and infrastructure in need of replacement, and there were signs on the horizon that the economy would be heading into a downturn. Our decentralized model was clearly wasteful and broken, and most importantly it placed our ability to sustain compliant systems at risk, so it was clear early in my role that we needed to centralize IT.

Because IT resources were scattered across the company, it was impossible to tackle more than a handful of major projects in any given year. The IT organization itself had evolved into a system with more managers than workers, leading to confusion over roles and responsibilities.

As external market conditions grew more difficult, Rich knew that the company would need a well-managed, tightly disciplined IT organization that was capable of delivering multiple projects on tight deadlines.

"We had to act like Mr. Wolf," Rich says with a chuckle, referring to a character in *Pulp Fiction* who calmly resolves a series of messy problems with unrelenting efficiency.

Over the next two years, we brought all of the IT professionals together into one global IT organization and we created a global IT methodology. It was challenging, but it was the right strategy for accomplishing the important results we were seeking, such as providing shared services across multiple business units and faster responses to shifting market conditions.

First, of course, we had to get senior-level buy-in starting at the CEO/CFO level so that everyone understood the business reason for consolidating IT. Then we put a process in place for identifying who would move into the global IT organization and who would stay with the business.

Consolidating IT was not easy; several leaders were worried that they would lose control, and many of the people targeted to move were worried about their careers. We put a governance model in place to allow the business to retain control over what IT did, and to ensure their needs were served.

For the individual, we implemented a new global career model, which simplified the number of levels and articulated what it takes to move to each level in the organization. We created a meritocracy based on results and global comparison of our talent to ensure people who delivered top results, no matter where they were located or who they reported to, were recognized for their contribution. This allowed us to reward people for their contributions, and it really "raised the bar" for our team, challenging our average players to step up their game.

Before we began our changes, 70 percent of my team was rated as performing in the top 20 percent, yet the business felt we provided minimal service to them. Our changes meant that some people had to hear the hard, honest truth that their contribution was average, when historically they, like almost all of their peers, were told they were superstars.

We saw some healthy turnover when we first made these changes, but we needed that to happen in order for our team to begin improving their performance. We had to teach the IT organization that the rest of the company expected us to act like service-focused professionals. And we had to keep the focus on our transformation, and not let people forget what we were trying to achieve.

From Pentagon to Pyramid

One of the largest challenges Rich faced was restructuring the shape of his organization. The IT organization Rich inherited looked more like a pentagon than a pyramid, with more senior managers and directors than junior managers.

"And it wasn't just the number of people at levels; the responsibilities assigned to each level were equally jumbled. We had senior managers and directors who managed no one or just a handful of people, while we had some managers who oversaw 100-plus people," says Rich.

This upside structure created serious issues for the IT organization, "with senior leaders really not leading," says Rich.

The old model also created career gridlock for people at lower levels, with top performers having no real way to advance their careers—"so they would leave the organization," says Rich.

To resolve this, Rich and his team tackled the roots of the problem, building a new simplified career model, streamlining job descriptions and job titles, rightsizing responsibilities with levels, dramatically reducing the use of experienced hire recruiting, and driving up college recruiting.

Rich also implemented changes that forced global perform-ance evaluation at all levels, driving a focus toward meritoc-racy where ratings are based on demonstrated results no matter where they live or whom they report up to.

"The results from these changes have been tremendous. We now truly know who our superstars are; they are re-warded for their efforts, and they move quickly," says Rich. "Our people also now get honest feedback on their perform-ance and understand what they need to do to progress or im-prove their performance rating."

Transforming IT was a difficult process, but it paid off. The introduction of a standard IT methodology, combined with the consolidation of the IT organization, gave Boston Scientific a critical advantage in the rapidly changing, highly complex mar-ket for advanced medical devices. "The business bought into our plan as soon as they saw the results," says Rich.

Three years ago, Rich implemented an IT governance board that includes BSC's leadership team. The governance board provides oversight on IT functions, prioritizing the ma-jor IT programs and recommending when IT spending and headcount should increase or decrease.

Elevated Perceptions

The business's response to the IT transformation at BSC has been clear. "We went from tackling a handful of major proj-ects in a year to completing 20 to 25 major projects annually," says Rich. "We went from being a company where nobody knew how to get what they needed from IT to being a company where we had a clearly defined process for getting IT projects started and finished. Most importantly, we went from being a team that only made it into the spotlight when things were broken to one that was proactive, well regarded, and had the opportunity to really make a difference."

Before this cultural transformation, almost all of the decisions related to IT were made by IT people, with little input from other people in the company. "In the past, a few IT folks would get together in a room and decide what they were going to do, and then they would tell the rest of the company what was going to happen," says Rich.

As a result, the business really felt powerless to get attention on the issues they most needed help resolving.

Today, we really want the business to make most of those decisions. The business should decide what they need from IT. We've tried hard to make the decision-making processes very transparent, so the business can see the costs and understand the priorities. This means as IT folks, we have to accept that sometimes the business will need less of our help and we will have to be flexible and confident enough to adapt as demand for our services increases or decreases.

Rich concedes that greater transparency has led to greater overall demand for IT services across the company. But it's also resulted in fewer requests from the business units for small projects or minor changes. That's good, says Rich, because it enables IT to concentrate on solving major challenges and developing solutions that can help the company grow its bottom line.

"Globalizing the IT organization and transforming ourselves into a service organization has allowed us to focus on providing innovation," says Rich. "We've become more than just a utility—now we're perceived as an engine for innovation. We bring new ideas to the table."

Rich uses another movie analogy to describe IT's new role in the enterprise: "We've expanded our mission to now focus on innovation in addition to delivering solutions, my team aspires to be like Q in the James Bond films. We devise solutions that people haven't thought of before, and we use technology to help people do their jobs more effectively."

In the not-so-distant past, Rich says, IT was "the last place you'd go for innovation. If the business made a suggestion, the IT guys would come up with a thousand reasons why that could not be done, such as, 'It will compromise security,' or 'It would violate regulations,' or 'We can't support it,' or 'It's not compatible with our systems.' Unfortunately, what happens is the business gets frustrated and needs help, so they go off and find a way to get it done anyway. Then the IT organization winds up having to support what becomes a key part of the business."

For example, an "old school" IT organization would probably sniff at the iPad and reject it. A modern IT organization is more likely to say, "Let's see what it can do." That's exactly the right approach for today's ultracompetitive economy, says Rich.

> *When the iPad was introduced, we immediately went out and bought 10 of them. It's not that we had a burning need for them, but we saw that the iPad had promise in helping our mobile professionals and our senior executives. So I pushed my team beyond the normal list of "why we can't" and we started a pilot project to test out iPads . . . we got out ahead of the curve.*
>
> *A few years ago, we would have crossed our arms and said, "No way, that's just a frivolous expensive toy. It doesn't run Windows. It won't stand up to the wear and tear of travel." Today we do the opposite. We recognize that it's a game-changer and we say, "How do we make this work for us? How do we support this new device?" . . . just like Q.*

Not all innovations are as inherently sexy as the iPad. For example, in-memory computing solutions don't have the popular appeal of the latest handheld devices, but they offer the potential of substantially faster data processing capabilities.

"With in-memory technology, you can grind away at the data much faster and bring information to the surface that never could have been found in years. So clearly this will be transformational, and we will start looking at it now to see how we can take advantage of this new technology," says Rich.

The IT organization plans to pilot small-scale projects to learn as much as possible about in-memory storage/

> "Globalizing the IT organization and transforming ourselves into a service organization has allowed us to focus on providing innovation. We've become more than just a utility—now we're perceived as an engine for innovation. We bring new ideas to the table."

databases—before it becomes the "hot new thing" that everyone suddenly needs to have. "Essentially, we're trying to be proactive instead of waiting for the business to come to us with a demand," Rich explains.

Organic Innovation

Rich says that he resisted the idea of setting up a special group within IT to lead innovation. I'll let Rich explain the rationale for this in his own words:

We take the same approach to innovation that we do to project management. I don't buy into the model where you create a specialized team for project management that was made popular by an academic group of IT analysts. We don't have a separate team of project management specialists because we want everyone at the manager and above level to be good project managers. Project management is central to our success, and we want those skills to be integrated throughout the IT organization.

For us, innovation has to be an organic activity. So we don't have a special group driving innovation. There's no "ivory tower" or "think tank" within IT. We want everyone in

IT to think of themselves as innovators, and we encourage everyone to bring their innovative ideas to the table.

The organization's organic approach to innovation has produced a steady stream of positive results in the form of new solutions for clinical applications, new programs for tracking payments to healthcare professionals, and a new enterprise-wide financial management system.

"It's been a sea change for all of us, and I'm delighted by our progress in this next step in our transformation," says Rich. "I am wildly proud of how my team has consistently made fundamental changes in the IT organization without disrupting our service to the business. Today the IT organization is perceived very differently than it was four years ago. We have evolved from a small, decentralized group of IT people who were 'the last ones you'd call' into a unified global team that generates tangible results for the business—and we're often called in first."

Establish the Baseline

Greg Buoncontri, the CIO of Pitney Bowes, considers himself a specialist in IT transformation. "It's what I do best," he says, "transforming an IT organization and giving it a new purpose, a new goal, and a new direction."

Not all IT transformations are alike, he notes, and they are undertaken for a variety of reasons. Sometimes an IT transformation follows a major transformation in the business itself, such as a merger or an acquisition. Sometimes the transformation is forced upon the organization by external circumstances, such as a major downturn in the economy, a significant tightening of the regulatory environment, or the introduction of a revolutionary new business model such as e-commerce.

"But there are always common elements," says Greg. "The most obvious reason for launching a transformation is simple: Whatever you are doing now isn't working very well. And usually there are compelling circumstances, a set of internal or external pressures that forces you to change."

A truly transformational CIO, he says, does more than just change the IT organization. "You've got to change the way people in the organization think, how they behave, how they measure success and keep score. You've got to change their world view."

In some cases, he adds, you also have to be ready to make personnel changes. Moving people around—or moving them out—can be painful. But sometimes it's necessary.

Under any circumstances, there are a series of preliminary steps that must be taken before beginning a transformation process.

The first step is establishing a good baseline. You have to know where you are today and understand how you're performing across multiple dimensions.

Then the second step is taking your baseline and applying it to figure out the gap between where you are and your "end

> "You've got to change the way people in the organization think, how they behave, how they measure success and keep score. You've got to change their world view."

state"—where you need to be when you finish your transformation.

The third step is setting milestones to measure your progress over the one, two, or three years it will take to complete your transformation.

It would be a serious mistake, says Greg, to assume that a transformation can be accomplished at warp speed. "That would be unrealistic. Sure, there might be some low-hanging fruit or some quick wins you can achieve to prove your credibility, but transforming an organization takes time, and it's not going to happen overnight. On the other hand, you can't allow the process to drag on for seven years."

Guiding a multiyear transformation requires genuine leadership skills, says Greg. "You need to explain to people why these changes have to be made and what things will look like when we all get to the other side. You have to describe the end state so people will understand what they're aiming for. You need to give people a 'north star' to follow. If everyone can keep that north star in mind, your transformation will have a better-than-average chance of succeeding."

Being a leader doesn't always mean having all the answers, he says. "It is perfectly acceptable to say, 'I'm not sure of every detail, but I know we're going to reach the end state we're aiming for and that we'll get there together.' That's why you need a baseline and an end state—so you know where you're going."

For example, when Greg joined Pitney Bowes, its IT functions were loosely organized. Like many decentralized IT organizations, it often responded to requests from individual business units by implementing individualized solutions. "But we had no common standards and no common approach for solving problems," says Greg. "Just sending an e-mail from one group to another could be difficult. We had so many help desks that people didn't know where to go for help. There was a lack of ownership and accountability."

As the market for the company's services became more competitive and more complex, a more unified IT strategy was required to optimize the use of resources, reduce duplication of effort, and prioritize project development. That meant transforming the IT organization.

From the perspective of the company's senior management, the desired end state was an IT organization that

Lesson

The transformation must be universal—it can't take place in a vacuum or be limited to just one part of the enterprise.

functioned as a shared service across the enterprise. "Our goal was creating a unified, cohesive organization that serves the company's business units, using common tools and standard techniques when practical, and providing unique solutions when necessary," Greg explains.

One of the first and most visible changes was the consolidation of the help desks. "We took nine help desks and collapsed them down to one," says Greg. "In the past, the help desks were closed on Sundays, and they only spoke one language. We turned the help desk into a 24/7 operation, speaking three languages."

Standardized, company-wide e-mail, desktop, HR, and payroll systems followed. The transformation process continued until IT could justifiably call itself a global organization serving the entire enterprise. "I would even like to think that some of the company's other shared services have learned something from our experiences," Greg says.

One of the key lessons of transformational IT strategy is that the transformation must be universal—it can't take place in a vacuum or be limited to just one part of the enterprise.

"Remember, when you transform IT, you also have to transform everything that touches IT. Your customers and your users have to change, too. You have to bring them through the transformation process with you. That means you need shared objectives and shared outcomes. It can't be 'heads I win, tails you lose.' Ideally, everyone should arrive at the end state together."

"You need to explain to people why these changes have to be made and what things will look like when we all get to the other side. You have to describe the end state so people will understand what they're aiming for. You need to give people a 'north star' to follow. If everyone can keep that north star in mind, your transformation will have a better-than-average chance of succeeding."

Riding Two Horses

There's a great scene in *The Mask of Zorro* in which the hero stands astride two galloping stallions to escape from his enemies. That scene came to mind midway through our conversation with Robin Johnson, the CIO of Dell.

Robin guided a transformation that changed the way IT and the business look at costs. And in the process, Dell reduced fixed IT costs by $160 million—and reinvested $100 million of the savings in development projects.

"More than half of our budget is now spent on building new value streams for Dell," says Robin. "That's radically different than what we were doing a couple of years ago."

What's truly amazing, in my opinion, is that Dell accomplished this miracle without increasing the IT budget or dramatically slashing programs. The extra money came from driving efficiency on what Robin calls "the fixed-cost side of the house."

When he joined Dell, Robin faced a challenge that is familiar to many CIOs: He could continue supporting costly legacy applications that people were comfortable using or he could shut the applications down and spend the money he saved on development projects.

Instinctively, he wanted to direct his resources toward development. But first he had to convince the business that the legacy apps were a significant problem.

Robin made his case in a variety of ways. For example, IT began charging the business units on a usage basis for each application. Now each business unit knew exactly how much it cost to run an application. That awareness of cost put the business units on the same page as IT.

"We aligned IT and the business to the goal of driving out cost. We got the business on our side. Now the business had an incentive to help us get rid of stuff that was no longer providing value," Robin explains.

In another instance, two business groups were using an inefficient ERP platform that could be replaced by newer and less expensive technology. IT convinced one group to migrate its operations to a newer system, but the other group wanted to stick with the old platform.

The old platform cost us $17 million a year to run and we charged each of the two groups $8.5 million a year to be on the platform. When one group committed to giving up the platform, we went to the second group and basically said, "Okay, *you're the last man on the platform so it's going to cost you $17 million a year to keep it running."*

When the second group considered how much extra revenue they would need to generate to cover the additional $8.5 million they would be charged for staying on the old platform, they agreed to make the change.

People later asked me, "How did you convince them to switch?" I said that part of it is about standing your ground, but that most of it is about explaining the actual costs of these platforms and putting it in a business perspective that everyone can easily grasp and understand.

It's actually pretty basic. It's like a reverse cost-benefit analysis. You start with the cost, then you find out the benefit they're hoping to achieve, and then you show them how they can achieve that benefit for less money.

As an experienced CIO, Robin also knew that even as they clung to their older systems, the business units would also demand the best new technologies so they could stay competitive in their rapidly evolving markets.

By getting the business units on board with IT's continuous cost reduction strategy, Robin could now offer them what amounted to a great deal: increased spending on development, accompanied by reduced (or flat) budgets for running costs.

"We focus very, very hard on things that allow us to take money out of the budget," says Robin. "And then we give the business the option of how to spend it."

From my perspective as a longtime observer of IT trends, that's another revolutionary step. In the past, IT probably would have figured out a way to keep the money it saved. At Dell, IT now perceives itself as an integral part of the enterprise—and it makes a real contribution to the overall financial picture.

> *That's how you establish credibility with the business. If the business helps us turn off a thousand old transactional systems and eliminate a thousand unnecessary reports, which then allows us to reduce the number of servers we need and reduce storage capacity—we say to the business "Okay, here's your savings. What would you like to do with the money?"*
>
> *It's very important that you are completely transparent with the business. Show them the savings and let* them *decide what to do with it.*

After showing the savings, Robin's team then takes the additional step of recommending where to invest the money.

> *We say, "Here are the next five things we can go do together that we guarantee will generate value. And we're pretty confident that following the recommended advice is going to yield additional savings and business benefits."*
>
> *We've discovered that when you take this approach, the business usually makes prudent decisions, based on common sense.*

Just imagine: an IT organization offering what amounts to a money-back guarantee! *That* is transformational.

It would be wrong, however, to suggest that Robin managed to wrestle all the cost-savings from the business. He also had to convince the IT organization that it could operate more efficiently, with fewer resources.

"It probably drives my people crazy, but I challenge them on every decision we make," says Robin. "For instance, if you run an infrastructure domain, I want to see your year-over-year plan and I ask you to show me how you're using technology to drive down your running costs while delivering like-for-like service. If you're running storage, I want to know if we're managing our application architectures appropriately to our SLAs. Are we tiering our storage? Are we archiving correctly? We're not likely to get a blank check to just increase capacity, so we're very keen on driving efficiency into everything we do."

Faster *and* Cheaper

Robin was not hired by Dell to be a ruthless cost-cutter. And he doesn't see himself as some kind of hyperefficient IT bean counter.

"I didn't come in with a cost-reduction mandate. In fact, the people in IT would have loved me if I had just kept the budget flat. It would have been a very popular decision within IT. A flat budget would have been considered a success—but it would have killed our credibility with the business units," he says.

He needed credibility with the business units to accomplish his real mission, which was helping the overall business—Dell Inc.—become more agile, more nimble, more responsive, and more successful in ultracompetitive markets all over the world.

This wasn't an isolated strategy. We didn't just say, "Hey, let's take $200 million out of costs." Our goal as an IT *organization was delivering solutions faster, extracting more value and more productivity for every development dollar that we spent.*

We knew that to accomplish this, we would need to standardize platforms. That, in turn, enabled us to reduce our costs, because standard platforms are simpler to support, simpler to operate, [and] require less software and fewer data centers.

So this whole strategy was really about speed and cost. That was a new one for me, because usually faster isn't cheaper. We all learned some important lessons here because this really is faster and cheaper.

As a bonus, the new approach to cost reduction freed up money that allowed the IT organization to pursue its real passion—developing exciting new technologies.

"Most of our people in IT want to work on things that are new and cool. They don't want to be writing 15 interfaces for the same app to 15 new backend databases," says Robin. "Most of us would like to develop something that creates new value and makes our customers happy."

Another benefit of standardizing is that it makes it easier for the development teams to create new software.

"For instance, instead of writing a separate interface for each customer database, we now only have to write one standard interface for a global customer database. As a result, we're creating better software, faster," says Robin. "We're delivering what the business wants, and we're doing it fast. That's why this is so exciting. We're getting a chance to do what we always really wanted to do."

IT at the Scrub Sink

Brian R. Lurie was recently promoted from a divisional CIO to vice president, global IT strategy and planning at Stryker Corporation, one of the largest medical technology companies in the world. In his new role, Brian will be responsible for leveraging ideas, talent, and capabilities across the company's 14 divisions.

I am certain that Brian will succeed, for two very good reasons:

1. He is a terrific, truly inspirational leader.

2. From his perch in IT, he had an unparalleled view into the inner workings of the enterprise.

Brian represents a new breed of transformational CIO, a smart and experienced leader who understands the company and its larger strategic issues.

"The successful CIO participates in the company's strategic discussions. But you won't be invited to those discussions unless the business leaders trust you and believe that you understand their customers. You gain that trust by delivering consistently on the basics and anticipating their needs. That's a given at any company."

> "The successful CIO participates in the company's strategic discussions. But you won't be invited to those discussions unless the business leaders trust you and believe that you understand their customers."

But it's what you do with the trust that you've earned that distinguishes ordinary CIOs from outstanding CIOs. Brian tells a great story about how the power of IT added value on the front lines:

I spend a lot of time with our customers, such as the surgeons who use the devices we make. Recently, a surgeon said to me, "Brian, I'm a busy guy." A little light bulb went on in my head. I wondered if we could educate our surgeon customers during the three minutes or so that it takes to scrub their hands.

I went back to my team in IT and I told them my idea. They came up with a handheld device that plays a short video that surgeons can watch while they are scrubbing. We call it our "Scrub Sink Presentation." It's an animation showing a new surgical technique. The device is held at eye level so the surgeon can watch it while he scrubs.

But here's the point of the story: I never would have thought of the idea unless I had been speaking with the surgeon, thanks to a strong partnership with the sales function at our company.

At Stryker, IT now participates in the product development process—a sure sign that a strong bond of trust that has grown between IT and the business.

Demystifying IT

Building trust between IT and the business is not an overnight process—it's a transformation that requires time, patience, and hard work.

"It happens in steps, and people are very skeptical. You have to remember that IT was traditionally viewed as a black hole—requests go in, but nothing comes out," says Brian. IT isn't just about cutting costs—it's also about generating revenue.

"Know the business better than the business knows the business."

Brian knew that the success of the company would depend on its ability to get new technology out into the market ahead of the competition—and he believed that IT could play a key role in that process.

In IT, we are our own worst enemies. We speak in acronyms and we convey an attitude that says, "Only we understand this technology." But then people go home and see their 10-year-old kid playing with technology that's more complex than what they're using at work.

So I never use acronyms. When I'm speaking with someone in the business, I try to be an educator, not an IT leader. There's not a day that goes by when I'm not extolling the role of technology and how it can benefit the business. Every conversation with a business leader creates an opportunity to change the way they perceive IT.

I also try to demystify IT whenever I can. A lot of people are frightened by IT, so they're leery. I try to explain that IT is just a process-focused approach to business—with steps that are very similar to any business process.

I think that if you spend enough time explaining IT to people, and if you consistently deliver on the basics, that you will win people over and they will invite you into the broader conversation.

It's also critical to link any discussions about IT with the real customer goals and objectives of the business. "You need to keep the focus on the business outcome. That has to be the driver," says Brian. "So when I'm talking to people in the business, I really do very little talking about IT. I do a lot of talking about business goals, and about the talent and resources it takes to accomplish those goals. I try to keep IT in the background of the discussion, albeit always an enabler."

Brian also shared some advice that every CIO should take to heart: "Know the business better than the business knows the business," he says. "As the CIO, you can be a great source of knowledge about the downstream impact of various plans and strategies, as IT looks across and is involved throughout the enterprise. But you have to know and understand the business. Then people will seek you out and ask you for your advice—because they know that you can see across the broad base of businesses and that you understand both the challenges and common goals."

Whatever you do, says Brian, do not allow IT to become a commodity in the enterprise.

The transformational CIO is someone who says, "I'm not going to live just in the IT world, I'm going to live across the enterprise."

> " . . . when I'm talking to people in the business, I really do very little talking about IT. I do a lot of talking about business goals, and about the talent and resources it takes to accomplish those goals. I try to keep IT in the background of the discussion, albeit always an enabler."

Chapter 3

Partnering with the Business

Executive Summary

As more critical business activities migrate to digital platforms, the relationship between IT and the business becomes more important than ever. While it's perfectly okay to use words such as *alignment*, *collaborative*, or *synergistic* when talking about this increasingly crucial relationship, the word that describes it best is *partnership*. As you will see in this chapter, the partnership between IT and the business takes many forms and is continually evolving. Managing this partnership is the CIO's highest priority.

Connecting at Multiple Levels

It's far easier to talk about partnering in the abstract than it is to actually form viable partnerships that deliver tangible benefits to IT and the business.

So we're reenlisting our friend Dave Smoley, the CIO at Flextronics, to walk us through the details of establishing partnerships that work in real-world situations. Dave is known in the industry for his ability to create and maintain partnerships with the business, so we decided to ask him directly for the "secret" of his success. Here is Dave's reply:

> *Partnering has to occur at multiple levels. That's really important. It can't just be at the top. A huge part of our success as an IT organization comes from partnering throughout the organization. It's definitely our top priority.*
>
> *At the CIO level, I partner in a number of different ways. The main way is by reaching out proactively and communicating with my peers in the business. They naturally tend to focus on a whole lot of stuff other than IT, so my communication with them has to be tailored to each individual's style, needs, interests, and responsibilities.*

That kind of communicating involves a fair amount of effort. With some people, you can take them out to dinner and spend an evening talking. And there are other people you can chase for weeks and you're lucky if you get a reply e-mail or a phone call. Each type of person presents a different tactical challenge.

One of the CIO's most important jobs is figuring out how to approach them in a way that is both engaging and helpful.

The rewards that flow from having good working relationships across the enterprise are usually worth the extra effort, says Dave. When people feel comfortable talking with you, and when they feel like they have a real relationship with you, they are more likely to come to you directly when they have an issue—and less likely to start shopping around for solutions outside of IT.

Dave makes a distinction between the informal activities that roll up into a network for good relationships and the formal activities that ensure alignment between IT and the business. One of the formal activities involves preparing an annual "State of the Business" review for each of the company's business units.

"Partnering has to occur at multiple levels. That's really important. It can't just be at the top. A huge part of our success as an IT organization comes from partnering throughout the organization."

Lesson

The rewards that flow from having good working relationships across the enterprise are usually worth the extra effort. When people feel comfortable talking with you, and when they feel like they have a real relationship with you, they are more likely to come to you directly when they have an issue—and less likely to start shopping around for solutions outside of IT.

These customized presentations usually include an overview of how IT is helping the business unit achieve its goals and objectives; a catalog of the applications, tools, and IT services used by the business unit; and a list of the unit's needs that IT is addressing or plans to address.

"Depending on the individual, I will deliver the review as a document or as part of a conversation," Dave explains. The key, he says, is knowing your audience—some people prefer reading a document, while others prefer listening to a presentation.

Again, Dave emphasizes that the end results make the additional efforts worthwhile.

I find that if you have the engagement and support at the top, then the rest of it becomes a lot easier. That alignment with senior management gives you synergy and momentum.

The other day I gave a 90-minute presentation to the CEO's staff. I basically reviewed everything that IT has accomplished over the past three years in terms of cost, performance, innovation, mistakes, opportunities, and outlook for the future. Then I follow up individually with the people who attended the meeting so I can get a better understanding of their perceptions and their needs. That's one of the ways you make the good high-level connections you need to lead a successful IT organization.

Dave also points out that organizational success requires more than establishing high-level connections between the CIO and his or her peers.

I've seen people flame out even when they have great relationships at the C-level and the staff level, because you also need to have great relationships with the business at many levels up and down your organization.

Our mission is making sure that every single person in the company has a "go-to" person in IT. For example, I'm the go-to guy for the C-level folks, but there are plenty of other important decision makers and key influencers in the business, and they also need their "go-to" person in IT.

IT uses a three-level matrix as the practical framework for achieving its close alignment with the business. The three levels are

1. Business unit

2. Functional

3. Region and site

Each business unit or segment leader has a corresponding IT segment leader. Each functional leader (finance, HR,

> "I basically reviewed everything that IT has accomplished over the past three years in terms of cost, performance, innovation, mistakes, opportunities, and outlook for the future. Then I follow up individually with the people who attended the meeting so I can get a better understanding of their perceptions and their needs."

engineering, manufacturing, etc.) has a corresponding IT senior director or director. Each site has an IT site leader reporting up through an IT regional leader.

In addition to staying in contact informally, the IT leaders are required to hold regular meetings with their corresponding managers in the business units and in the various functional areas of the company. "In some cases it's a formal staff meeting, in other cases it's a phone call just to touch base," Dave explains.

The overarching goal, says Dave, is making it nearly impossible for anyone to fall through the cracks.

You've got a matrix covering the business units, the functional areas and the sites and regions. That way, everybody in the company knows who to call when they need help from IT.

People might get mad at you when something doesn't work, but as long as they're talking to you and you're talking to

> ### Lesson
>
> Dave makes a distinction between the informal activities that roll up into a network for good relationships and the formal activities that ensure alignment between IT and the business. One of the formal activities involves preparing an annual "State of the Business" review for each of the company's business units.

them, everything will be okay. That's our goal—always keeping those lines of communication open and the conversation going. Because when you don't hear anything or when they quit talking to you—that's when you really have to worry.

The "Outsider"

If you ask Tony Scott, the CIO at Microsoft, to describe what he likes best about the growing partnership between IT and the business, he'll tell you it's the closer collaboration with the company's product groups.

Traditionally, the IT organization here would test products as they were going through various phases of the development cycle. But now we're involved in the product design. We're involved with our product groups way up front and we're influencing the features that get into the products supporting large enterprises.

We help the product groups make sure that our new products have the features that big companies really want, such as manageability, upgradeability, and low cost of support. That's where we're making the biggest contribution.

"Traditionally, the IT organization here would test products as they were going through various phases of the development cycle. But now we're involved in the product design."

Any time you can influence your company's products in a positive way—not just testing them, but having a direct influence on the quality and the direction and the capabilities of the products—that's the ultimate value you can provide.

When you listen to Tony talking about the collaboration between IT and the product groups, you can hear the excitement in his voice. From Tony's perspective, the difference between testing and designing is like the difference between riding a scooter and riding a motorcycle!

The tighter relationship between IT and the business didn't blossom overnight. It helped that Tony was considered an outsider, since he had not worked previously for Microsoft. It also helped that in his previous roles at major companies, such as General Motors and Disney, he had been a Microsoft customer.

As a customer, he had earned a reputation for being tough, but fair. That reputation, combined with his outsider status, imbued Tony with the street cred he needed to win the confidence of both the IT organization and the business.

"One of the advantages I had coming in from the outside was that I knew most of the senior product executives and I had interacted with them in a positive way when I was a customer," Tony explains. "So they could say, 'He's okay, that's what he does,' to the people who didn't know me. That definitely helped."

Tony also had to convince the IT organization that working more closely with the business was worth the extra effort. Tony used a three-pronged approach to win hearts and minds within the IT group.

First, I had to make it clear to the people in IT that we had an opportunity, a vision, and a strategy. I had to reinforce the importance of our role and show them how a closer working relationship with the business would benefit them.

Second, we had to set performance criteria so we could measure individual levels of participation and collaboration in an objective way.

Third, we had to formally engage with the product groups and define our measure of success. We had to create shared goals and then figure out how to measure ourselves based on our actual achievement of those shared goals.

So those were the three parts: the overall strategy, the individual measure of performance, and the organizational scorecard that told us if we had met the business goals we had established.

As it turned out, one of Tony's hardest tasks was keeping the business groups aware of the risks they faced when they relied on newer technologies to achieve their goals.

We all want to be high achievers, but you also have to think about the risks involved with emerging technologies that don't have a proven track record. So you have to explain the risk and create a backup plan and establish key decision points along the way, so that if things start going badly, you can recover.

> "I had to make it clear to the people in IT that
> we had an opportunity, a vision, and a strategy.
> I had to reinforce the importance of our role
> and show them how a closer working relation-
> ship with the business would benefit them."

You have to explain all those things. You can't just shake your head and say, "Well, you're on your own." That's not a partnership.

Tony sees the partnership between IT and the business evolving slowly and gradually. "It's a journey that we're still on. I think it will be something that plays out over time. We see some good signs and some trouble spots, but we're hopeful for positive results."

As the partnership evolves, the role of the CIO will evolve, too. New synergies seems to be emerging between IT, sales, and marketing—due mostly to the adoption of newer digital technologies by those functional areas. Here is Tony's take on the changing relationships among the principal players in the corporate game board:

As more and more of a company's interactions with its customers take place in some kind of digital media, you will need tighter alignments between IT, sales, and marketing to maintain the brand vision, the brand promise, and the brand execution. In the past, when everything was analog, they were pretty disconnected. In a digital world, they have to be joined much more closely together.

In the past, for example, the CMO probably didn't pay a lot of attention to IT. But if I were the CMO of a sizable company today, I would want the smartest person in IT on my staff as one of my direct reports. And I would want my best friend in the company to be the CIO.

Transitioning to Global Leadership

Jay Crotts is vice president of IT Services at Shell Oil. When I asked him to chat about the role of senior IT executives in global corporations, he gently reminded me that not every company that calls itself global operates as a global enterprise.

The truly global enterprise is more than just a collection of businesses located in various parts of the world. The truly global enterprise strives toward developing common global strategies for delivering its products and services to *real* customers in *real* markets—wherever they are.

In a truly global enterprise, IT plays an absolutely critical role by enabling and supporting that global delivery strategy on a 24/7 basis. In a sense, IT becomes one big global solution, and IT executives become global leaders.

Lesson

The growth of e-business and all of the newer digital customer interfaces means that in many situations, IT has become the company's face. That puts a different kind of responsibility on the CIO's shoulders.

For some CIOs, the transition to a global leadership role has been tricky. But Jay sees it somewhat differently. I'll let him describe the changing role of the CIO in his own words:

> *The CIO's basic responsibilities haven't changed radically since the role emerged 20 or 30 years ago. The CIO is still responsible for integrating IT into the business strategy, translating business strategy into IT outcomes, and ensuring that IT is efficient and effective.*
>
> *The challenge now is that the world is changing fast and as a result, business is changing fast.*
>
> *Now there's a lot riding on the CIO's ability to adapt to all of those changes. Some of the changes involve technology and innovation. Most CIOs are comfortable dealing with those kinds of changes.*
>
> *But the real challenge for CIOs comes from the rapid globalization of the economy. Globalization means that CIOs have to deliver solutions supporting business operations all over the world, from Paris to Pakistan.*
>
> *It would be great if we could approach every market in a unified way, and it would be really nice if the world around us never changed, but that's not today's reality.*

Because each market is different and because each market evolves at a different pace, the alignment between IT and the business will never be perfect. But that doesn't let the CIO off the hook, says Jay.

> *The company now depends on you even more than you ever realized. The company relies on you to adapt your resources to changing business strategies, and to deliver effective solutions, in many markets, worldwide.*

> ### Lesson
>
> The CIO's basic responsibilities haven't changed radically since the role emerged 20 or 30 years ago. The CIO is still responsible for integrating IT into the business strategy, translating business strategy into IT outcomes, and ensuring that IT is efficient and effective.

The growth of e-business and all of the newer digital customer interfaces means that in many situations, IT has become the company's face. That puts a different kind of responsibility on the CIO's shoulders.

As Jay suggests, IT has become the primary point of contact between many companies and their customers. Please stop and think about this for a moment. Twenty years ago, people who predicted that IT would play a leading role in maintaining and supporting customer relationships were largely dismissed as visionary fools with little understanding of sales, marketing, and service—the primary and certainly the most important customer-facing activities at most companies.

Being Where the Strategy Is Set

The word *strategy* is almost always associated with the highest levels of the business. After all, isn't it the CEO's job to set strategy? The answer is yes—in theory. But in reality, business strategy is set at several levels, most of them below the C-suite.

It's crucial for the CIO to grasp this central reality of business and to create an IT presence at the various tables at

> ## Lesson
>
> The truly global enterprise is more than just a collection of businesses located in various parts of the world. The truly global enterprise strives toward developing common global strategies for delivering its products and services to *real* customers in *real* markets—wherever they are.

which strategy is discussed and developed. Basically, that means you need a process for matching IT people with the company's various business units. Jay describes the challenge and offers some great advice:

> *It's important for IT staff to be where the strategy is set. It would be great if every business person would come to you and say, "I have an idea and I think we need IT to be involved, please help." Sometimes that conversation happens, but most of the time, that conversation doesn't take place or takes place much later than it should have.*
>
> *That's the challenge you face: putting the right number of IT people with the right set of talents where the business strategies are set. I would say that your ability to assign those IT people correctly is paramount. This is something you really need to get right.*
>
> *Let me put it this way: I can get a lot of people to help me run operations and I can get a lot of people to help me run projects. But what's hard is making sure that I have the right person who is going to be there with the business, from beginning to end, to ensure that we deliver that business strategy successfully, and then continue to refine and improve what we're doing.*

Lesson

It's crucial for the CIO to grasp this central reality of business and to create an IT presence at the various tables at which strategy is discussed and developed. Basically, that means you need a process for matching IT people with the company's various business units.

That's the model that I start with and it's absolutely essential . . . and it's an area where I see many companies making mistakes. They'll let a consultant do the business interface work, or they won't have enough capable staff . . . and then you can get into very difficult situations.

Properly matching IT staff with the company's many business units can be a time-consuming task, but ensuring the right match-ups is worth the extra effort, says Jay.

Fundamentally, we look at the organizational structure of the business unit and its P&L [profit and loss]. We figure out who is ultimately accountable for the P&L, and then we assign the right talent to be the "face" of IT for the business. It's likely that these people will need a small organization underneath them . . . but the organization shouldn't be really large, because you want your people to focus on business strategy and end-to-end IT, not on delivering operations.

This, I believe, is a crucial point that tends to be overlooked or just plain misunderstood. As Jay rightly notes, the role of business-facing IT staff is making sure that IT is aligned with business strategy. Their jobs are less about delivering operational results and more about delivering business results.

> "That's the challenge you face: putting the right number of IT people with the right set of talents where the business strategies are set."

In other words, you don't assign IT people to business units so they can run IT operations; you assign IT people to business units so they can help the business units achieve their business objectives. This is an important distinction, and I am delighted that Jay took the time to discuss it with us in detail.

The business doesn't really care about the IT details. They expect you to deliver the operational piece.

I depend on IT people who are strategically placed in the business to translate business requirements into IT strategy, as well as enabling IT. That's how IT really helps the business. At a big company, it's all about moving markets. The technology is one component of a larger strategy.

What's *Really* Important to the Business?

One of the best management techniques for developing and maintaining good partnerships between IT and the business is by formally linking IT systems to business key performance indicators (KPIs). That usually means going beyond the standard conversation with a business leader who tells you that all he or she cares about is growing revenue and improving profitability. You have to be willing to probe, dig, and investigate—like a good detective!

"You need to find out what's *really* important to the business," says Jay. "Everyone immediately says revenue growth and profit. But typically there are five to ten underlying measures that most business people focus on. So you really have to work with the various businesses to find out what those measures are."

In some business units, for example, *on time and in full* delivery of products to customers is a critical KPI, because the customers literally can't do any work if the products aren't where they're supposed to be. A quick scan of the unit's balance sheet might not reveal this crucial fact. But the IT talent assigned to the business unit should be capable of digging beneath the surface, discovering what the unit really needs, and relaying that information to senior IT management so it can be translated into an operational strategy. Jay explains how this works in the real world:

Once you've found the KPIs that are important to the business, then your next step is figuring out which IT systems are needed to support those KPIs. For example, in the lubricants business there are probably eight critical systems that must be integrated and running to support the "on time and in full" KPI.

Another example: "Stock outs" are obviously an important KPI in the aviation fueling business. But invoice accuracy also drives customer satisfaction levels in that business. There are about a dozen IT systems involved in the process of ensuring invoice accuracy. Those systems must be integrated and operational to support the business's need to generate accurate invoices for its customers.

"You need to find out what's *really* important to the business. Everyone immediately says revenue growth and profit. But typically there are five to ten underlying measures that most business people focus on. So you really have to work with the various businesses to find out what those measures are."

The net takeaway here is that each business unit is likely to have its own set of KPIs, and that different sets of IT tools might be required to support those different sets of KPIs. When it comes to provisioning various business units within the company, you just cannot assume there is a one-size-fits-all solution.

The ability of IT to understand this fundamental concept, and to act in concert with the larger strategy, enables the company to capitalize on opportunities and gain competitive advantages. For example, Shell recently decided, for a variety of prudent business reasons, to close most of its operations in a foreign market. Through tight partnership between IT and the business, the company was able to maintain its presence in the market through distributors and an e-business portal. "We have a virtual presence which enables our customers there to order products and arrange delivery, in their native language, through a network of distributors," Jay explains.

Basically, the company exited a direct market *without* sacrificing that market's sales revenue. As a bonus, the company's

> ## Lesson
>
> The net takeaway here is that each business unit is likely to have its own set of KPIs, and that different sets of IT tools might be required to support those different sets of KPIs. The ability of IT to understand this fundamental concept, and to act in concert with the larger strategy, enables the company to capitalize on opportunities and gain competitive advantages.

cost of doing business in that market dropped dramatically. The secret to this success was the close working relationship between IT and the business.

In one instance, IT developed a workaround when the telecom links between the company and its retailers in a European country briefly went down. The telecom links were critical for verifying the validity of credit cards used by drivers when they purchased gasoline.

"In the old days, a lot of CIOs didn't understand the business. They thought IT was all about projects. Today, IT is all about the business. We feel an emotional connection to the business, we feel part of the business, and we want to support the needs of the business," says Jay. "Our goal is for the business to see us as a trusted partner that happens to specialize in IT."

When a guy like Jay says, "I'm very passionate about IT's engagement with the business," you know that he really means it.

The Age of Immediacy

When I was a younger man, I had a vision of the future. In my imagination, the future was a gleaming, pristine community of parks, lakes, and buildings, neither city nor suburb, bustling with human energy, but never so crowded or so noisy as to seem oppressive. It was mostly a place of peace, tranquility, and harmony.

I think I got the "bustling with human energy" piece of the vision right. The "peace, tranquility, and harmony" part now seems a bit off the mark. Instead of making our lives easier and less complicated, many of our newer technologies have had the opposite effect: We're busier and more harried than ever.

That's not necessarily a bad thing. Frankly, most of us would rather be busy than bored. But for those of us who make our living in the IT space, the newer technologies are having an impact that few of us were able to foresee.

Now that everyone, it seems, has some kind of smartphone and access to a high-speed Internet connection, the pace of

> "In the old days, a lot of CIOs didn't understand the business. They thought IT was all about projects. Today, IT is all about the business. We feel an emotional connection to the business, we feel part of the business, and we want to support the needs of the business. Our goal is for the business to see us as a trusted partner that happens to specialize in IT."

life has really picked up dramatically. You all know what I'm talking about, so there's no point in belaboring it.

From a business perspective, the broad adoption of these newer technologies has accelerated the demand for newer services. This rapidly accelerating demand for new services is placing a new set of burdens on IT.

We recently asked Stephen Savage, the CIO at CA Technologies (formerly Computer Associates), to chat with us about the evolving relationship between IT and the business. At one point in the conversation, we asked him to describe what the business expects from IT. Here is Stephen's answer:

> *If you had asked me that question a year ago, I would have answered you completely differently than the way I'm going to answer you today. What the business expects from IT is now. There's very little patience for any kind of delay in the delivery of whatever it is that the business is looking for—they want it instantaneously.*

This sense of impatience and entitlement is now part of our culture, thanks in no small part to all of the handy digital devices that we use continuously during a typical day.

> *Think of your iPhone and the fact that you can download an application and be up and running with it in seconds. That kind of speed now seems normal, and you now expect it. Well, that same expectation carries over into the business world.*
>
> *The idea of six-month or nine-month release cycles with these behemoth application systems that we've grown to love and hate over the years is less appetizing.*

"Think of your iPhone and the fact that you
can download an application and be up and
running with it in seconds. That kind of speed
now seems normal, and you now expect it.
Well, that same expectation carries over into
the business world."

Today, the operative word is now. *Especially in situations
where you can have not* all, *but* most *of the functionality you
want, and it's close enough to get you up and running* now,
as opposed to later.

In this kind of scenario, the CIO needs to act as a traffic
cop, making sure that demands for new technologies
and new systems don't create more headaches than they
solve.

"Clearly, you've got governance issues that come into
play," says Stephen. "You need to decide which services to
put in the cloud and which services you continue to operate
internally. You need to determine the risk profile and figure
out what would happen if there's a security breach."

All valid points, to be sure. But in today's environment—in
the Age of Immediacy—the CIO can't afford to be seen as a
naysayer. If you don't find a way to work *with* the business,
the business just might find a way to work without you. At
many companies, you will hear stories of business units that
went ahead and purchased technology after losing patience
with the IT department.

> # Lesson
>
> Partner with eager champions within the business to promote new technologies—and make certain that the decision-making process for acquiring new technologies is fair, honest, and transparent.

"That just opens the door to 'shadow IT,' which is really the last thing you want in today's world," Stephen cautions.

Like several of the more experienced executives we interviewed, Stephen advises CIOs to partner with eager champions within the business to promote new technologies—and to make certain that the decision-making process for acquiring new technologies is fair, honest, and transparent.

"You really need a good governance process so you can deliver the services that the business needs rapidly and safely," says Stephen, echoing the concerns of many CIOs struggling to find a middle ground between absolute control and complete abandon. "As a company, we have recognized that IT governance *does* matter. We have a great management team that respects the need for governance, and, at the same time, is impatient for change."

As part of its governance process, CA Technologies established two formal committees, the Investment Council and the Integration Council, to safeguard the integrity of the company's IT assets.

Basically, the Integration Council protects the IT architecture. The Investment Council governs the amount of money we will spend and decides policy issues associated with IT activities. We run all ideas and all proposals through these two bodies, which meet frequently enough so they don't stop the business from moving ahead quickly.

Senior management is represented on both committees. The Investment Council includes the chief financial officer (CFO), the chief operating officer (COO), the chief information officer (CIO) and the chief administrative officer (CAO), who also chairs the committee. The Integration Committee includes senior members from each of the principle areas of the business—sales, marketing, development, support, and finance—and it is chaired by the CIO.

The governance process affords an opportunity for all ideas to work themselves through a funnel and to be prioritized, with full transparency, so the business leaders can weigh the pros and cons and see for themselves which ideas will bear the most fruit. The process looks carefully at risks and rewards, enabling us to place the best bets for the future.

Lesson

As part of its governance process, CA Technologies established two formal committees, the Investment Council and the Integration Council, to safeguard the integrity of the company's IT assets. " . . . The Integration Council protects the IT architecture. The Investment Council governs the amount of money we will spend and decides policy issues associated with IT activities. We run all ideas and all proposals through these two bodies, which meet frequently enough so they don't stop the business from moving ahead quickly."

When we suggested that the company's process for assessing risks and rewards was perhaps elevating IT governance to a "science," Stephen didn't hesitate to set us straight.

> *Science? No, it's still subjective. And that's the way it should be. We will entertain requests with soft ROIs. You take, for instance, the Enterprise 2.0 initiative that we've launched across the organization. It's basically a Facebook-like collaboration tool that fosters better collaboration on projects and improved teamwork across the organization.*
>
> *It was difficult to place a hard ROI on it, but we still funded the initiative because we believed that it will serve the long-term interests of the corporation by attracting new people and promoting a mobile workforce.*
>
> *We also knew that if we didn't have a collaborative working environment for employees that are highly mobile, we would actually limit our ability to foster innovation in the organization.*
>
> *How do you measure that? In the near term, it's hard to say. Long-term, we believe it was a good bet.*

"You really need a good governance process so you can deliver the services that the business needs rapidly and safely. . . . We have a great management team that respects the need for governance, and, at the same time, is impatient for change."

New Convergence

If you haven't had a chance to hear Marc Benioff speak, you're missing an interesting experience. Benioff, as most of you already know, is the founder and CEO of Salesforce.com, the company that brought software as a service (SaaS) to the masses. I was sitting in the front row at one of the company's Cloudforce events in Manhattan recently, listening to Marc speak. I was impressed by his energy and exuberance.

He radiated a sort of visionary optimism that reminded me of the 1990s. But it suited him well, and he won over the audience with his descriptions of a world in which the traditional enterprise software model had been effectively replaced by a hybrid of cloud, mobile, and social computing.

After Marc and his colleagues finished speaking, the audience rose to its feet and applauded wildly. It felt more like a rock concert than a vendor presentation. As I looked around the packed room, I noticed only a handful of senior IT people. Their absence made sense; it occurred to me that many of Salesforce.com's products and services are probably sold directly to business units, bypassing the IT procurement process. If that's indeed the case, then I can understand why some CIOs might feel uncomfortable listening to Marc evangelize about a world without enterprise software.

But it would be a major mistake to dismiss Marc as some kind of speculative digital prophet. Marc knows exactly what he's talking about: the newest and most radical convergence of technology platforms to occur in the Information Age.

This new convergence of cloud, mobile, and social computing is already happening. If you don't believe Marc, ask the folks at IBM, Microsoft, Apple, Dell, Sony, SAP, Cisco, Red Hat, and other major innovators in the information technology industry.

Marc's vision of the future might not be dead-on perfectly accurate, but even if he's reasonably close in his assessment, we need to pay attention. Marc is one of the people in this industry who truly sees the big picture, and that's why we're closing this chapter with an unedited interview that we conducted with him via e-mail.

Unedited Interview with Marc Benioff

Hunter: As CEO, what do you expect from the IT team in terms of guiding innovation and helping the business accelerate demand creation?

Marc: I expect a lot! IT is a key platform for growth—and it is increasingly being recognized by businesses of all sizes as such.

Lesson

This new convergence of cloud, mobile, and social computing is already happening. If you don't believe Marc, ask the folks at IBM, Microsoft, Apple, Dell, Sony, SAP, Cisco, Red Hat, and other major innovators in the information technology industry.

At the most basic level, IT teams are responsible for one of a business's most core assets—its information. IT is not about running a cost center, or keeping up with the maintenance of legacy systems; that's antiquated, as everything is going to the cloud. The best IT teams use technology as a competitive advantage and play a significant strategic role in the growth of an organization. Basically, I expect an IT team to help a company out-innovate and out-execute its competition.

Unfortunately, not all IT teams fully leverage the opportunity they have. Recently I talked to more than 60 CIOs in various meetings throughout America's heartland. I spoke to them about the fundamental shift underway in our industry. I shared how we are moving from Cloud 1, which was about low cost, ease of use, and speed (and has transformed how companies use IT over the past 10 years) to Cloud 2, which is about collaboration, new mobile devices, and real time— which will change everything even more profoundly. With new mobile devices and the social revolution, the world has changed, I told them, and I shared how this new paradigm will define computing for the next 10 years.

> " . . . we are moving from Cloud 1, which was about low cost, ease of use, and speed . . . to Cloud 2, which is about collaboration, new mobile devices, and real time—which will change everything even more profoundly. With new mobile devices and the social revolution, the world has changed . . . "

The problem? Not only are some not ready for this transformation, but many of them hadn't even made it to Cloud 1 yet—some are still on mainframes. They are working on MVS/CICS, or Lotus Notes (which is so old it was conceived before Facebook founder Mark Zuckerberg, the father of the social revolution). They have never heard of Cocoa, or even that there is now HTML5. This is unacceptable. The next generation is here and every CIO must go faster. Unfortunately, there are some CIOs who would rather retire than go faster. And, if that's the case, they should. The CIO role—and the necessity to pursue IT through a lens of innovation and competitiveness—is more important, and the opportunities are more exciting, than ever before.

Hunter: In a perfect world, what role would the IT team play in supporting product development and marketing?

Marc: In a perfect world—and in the best examples—it's a truly integrated role. IT is a pivotal aspect of any modern business and the IT decision makers must consider—and be considered—in all areas of business development and marketing. It used to be that technologies were operational, and focused on the internal aspects of a business. At some point we referred to some of these things as back office, but IT is not back office. It's front and center. It's core.

IT is a competitive weapon. Technology is needed to leverage information, execute strategy, make the best business decisions, and generate revenue. That means that it can't exist in a silo, but IT teams must work across the organization.

For many companies (and certainly at Salesforce.com), IT plays a critical role as the "best" customer for the products being developed. And as an early adopter, IT should partner with R&D [research and development] to more rapidly iterate to change and improve all products. At our company, the IT team meets monthly with the Product team to submit product enhancements and help influence the product road map. IT should also play a critical role in helping product development and marketing get to market faster with the early adoption of the latest real-time technologies and the use of iterative delivery models.

I hear many great stories from our customers. Let me give you one example of how Starbucks innovatively used IT to make a positive impact on customer engagement, product development, marketing, and revenue. The company was looking for a dynamic way to engage with its customers. It launched My Starbucks Idea (powered by Salesforce Ideas functionality) in just six weeks. CEO Howard Schultz commented in *BusinessWeek* that the tool changed his company by installing "a seeing culture." By using innovative technology to help track the best ideas, the company launched new products and services, including free AT&T Wi-Fi access for iPhone users, a more robust hot chocolate, and its ready-brew instant coffee VIA.

Hunter: Can you offer some examples of how the IT team has made significant contributions to the business?

Marc: It's everywhere in our business—we are a technology company dedicated to making people successful by managing their most valuable information in the most efficient, secure, productive, collaborative, and real-time manner. What I'm most excited about now is our new product called Chatter, which is an enterprise-wide app for collaboration, and which has already changed the way our company works. People with expertise and experience are instantly looped in and participate in conversations, collaborate, and make contributions more simply than ever before. I have awareness about what's happening with employees, customers, products, customer service escalations, deals that are closing. Chatter changed everything. E-mail is down more than 43 percent within our organization. And, through this new way of communicating that is based on feeds and groups and collaboration, I now know more about my company in the past month than I have in the last three years. Amazingly, I've done it all from my iPhone, which means that it no longer matters if I am home, at the office, or Starbucks, I am productive wherever I am.

Let me give you another example of how the IT team of one of our customers made an incredible contribution to a very large organization. Japan Post Network, the world's largest institution in terms of asset holdings, needed to create an exclusive system that integrated those of the three existing companies. It wanted to consolidate paper-based customer data and feedback and needed a way to issue timely reports to the group companies. It needed to compile a database of personal information usage agreements with customers that also supported cross-selling opportunities between the different group companies.

This was a huge undertaking. Every person in Japan would be moved to this system. And, Kazuhiko Yoshimoto, the CIO at the time, demonstrated amazing insight, innovation, and courage when he supported the move to the cloud computing model over the traditional model. The result was extraordinary. Using our cloud computing platform Force.com, they built custom apps and developed a system that fully met their needs in cost and functionality in two months. They also gained development productivity, flexibility, and the ability to change things easily. Now Japan Post's 70,000 users can easily access the application via an Internet browser from any of the 24,000 offices, and management now has real-time visibility into business processes using reports and the dashboard.

In yet another case, Avon, a company that is 125 years old, is currently reenergizing its entire model with the implementation of innovative IT. The business has a goal to basically double its business in five years. And, a significant piece of that will be driven from initiatives CIO Donagh Herlighy is championing.

Hunter: Why is it important for IT to understand the customer experience and work closely with the business to enrich the customer experience?

Marc: Any part of a business must understand the customer and contribute to making the customer experience the best it can possibly be; of course IT is no exception. In our industry, we've seen for too long that software development was portioned off from the end user. This doesn't work.

One must always think about the customer experience. We saw this from the beginning of how we developed our service to be easy and fun for our customers and we see it in how we use our service to reach existing and new customers. We follow up with prospective customers in 24 hours. And we are committed to making all of them successful. Our technology and the attention of our IT teams to support the rest of the business is what enables us to execute on that value.

We've found the tremendous value of prototyping (which is very easy with our platform, Force.com) and the need for IT to sit with the business to define and change, in real time, the customer experience. The technologies we have today don't require the business to define the needs up front; it's a collaborative, iterative process—and IT makes this possible.

Today's CEOs are looking for their CIOs to be closer to the end customer, and that means CIOs need to understand all aspects of the business process and the levers for business model success. The line between the internal and external customer is going away. Innovative CIOs aren't waiting for business requirements; they are leading the business to rapidly execute on roadmaps, deliver, and accelerate value.

Hunter: How does top management ensure that IT understands the customer perspective and works closely with the business to achieve high levels of customer satisfaction?

Marc: At our company, our biggest priority is customer success. Everyone who works at Salesforce.com knows this.

Lesson

CEOs are looking for their CIOs to be closer to the end customer and that means CIOs need to understand all aspects of the business process and the levers for business model success. The line between the internal and external customer is going away. Innovative CIOs aren't waiting for business requirements; they are leading the business to rapidly execute on roadmaps, deliver, and accelerate value.

Communication is one of the most important parts of my job—and communicating the value of customer success is my most important message. We run our business with a management tool I invented called V2MOM. It's an acronym for Vision, Values, Methods, Obstacles, and Measures, and by having everyone within the organization assigning ideas to each of these, and prioritizing them, and being responsible for them, we ensure that we are all aligned.

Hunter: What skills does the CIO need to maintain close alignment between IT and the business?

Marc: CIOs need to innovate, improve the ROI [return on investment] of IT, and deliver business value—fast. To do all of those things, a CIO needs vision, leadership, business and technical acumen, and an ability to collaborate, communicate, and inspire change.

In the leadership chapter of my book, *Behind the Cloud*, I write that the number-one skill we look for in a new hire is a desire to change the world. That's especially true for a CIO. In this world that is rapidly changing, CIOs have to be ready to see change, evangelize it, inspire the senior management team, and bring the future into their organizations.

I recently hosted a dinner in New York for some of our biggest customers. One of the CIOs of a very prominent company, when introducing himself, joked about what the letters in his CIO title stood for—Career Is Over. This saying has been circulating for some time. Being a CIO requires being a change agent, and that often means being the bearer of bad news. Today's CIOs are charged with bringing problems with antiquated systems to the attention of the senior team—and having the task to explain why these expensive, but innovation-less, systems must now be replaced—and why an investment in IT must be made, even though budgets are tight. The best management teams get it, but others don't.

Today's CIOs must be hyper-aware of the rapidly changing landscape and be patient educators and communicators as they help their companies walk (or even better, run) through a new door that has opened. They must demonstrate the value of the initiative on the business and they must have strong relationships and networks up and down and across the organization.

I think in this new paradigm it's easier and more exciting than ever, but it does take a visionary perspective and the willingness to be a bit of a rebel to bring change to an organization. With those skills, CIO stands for Career Is ON (to

Lesson

CIOs need to innovate, improve the ROI of IT, and deliver business value—fast. To do all of those things, a CIO needs vision, leadership, business and technical acumen, and an ability to collaborate, communicate, and inspire change.

something big), as innovative IT will result in a profound impact on the business.

Hunter: Can you offer an example of how IT has taken a leadership role in achieving a customer-focused business objective or helped the business improve the customer experience?

Marc: Sure, one of our most recent examples is the launch of our new Help Portal, where we used Salesforce Sites, Knowledge Base and platform technologies, to deliver a Help Portal that radically improved the customer self-service online help experience and the customer service center productivity.

Another good example, in which we've seen significant results, is our Ideas platform. We have been on a constant quest to grow our customer community, and we build offline and online forums to do so. A number of years ago we launched a web site for customers who successfully self-implemented our service, as a way for them to share their experiences with others using the service or with those considering it. As technologies developed and the social revolution grew, we began to experiment with blogs, message boards, and other forms of social media. It wasn't long before we had tens of thousands of customers giving advice—and we needed a way to take advantage of this phenomenon.

Calling upon crowd-sourcing models and web sites like Digg, which allow users to share, discover, and vote on content, we created the ability for customers to vote on and rate ideas posted by the community, and it offered us a way to introduce an idea and observe how it resonated with our customer community. The site became, as Jamie Grenney, our Ideas product manager, likes to call it, "a global focus group that never sleeps."

This changed our business, and soon we offered it as a product to help other businesses. I've already shared with you how Starbucks uses it, and Dell's IdeaStorm provides another interesting example. IdeaStorm was built (in three weeks) to give Dell customers and enthusiasts a chance to become a part of the product development process. The day the site launched, a user suggested that Dell sell computers with the Linux platform preinstalled. In the coming weeks, tens of thousands of users agreed, and the post ranked as the number-one idea for months. Three months later, as a direct result of this intelligence, Dell released several consumer notebooks and desktops with the Linux operating system preinstalled—with the help of information technology, the company knew exactly what its customers wanted.

Chapter 4

The Art and Science of IT Leadership

Executive Summary

The term *change management* has been thrown around loosely for years, but until fairly recently, the CIO was rarely a key player in companywide transformation efforts. Today, the CIO is likely to be right in the middle of any major transformational initiative. As a result, the CIO's leadership skills will be stretched and tested to a far greater degree than ever before.

A Continuous Process of Engagement

Over the course of writing this book, we interviewed dozens of executives, managers, analysts, and industry experts. We began with the notion that if we spoke with enough people, we would discover the secret to guiding successful IT transformations.

Instead we discovered something more valuable. We discovered that leading a successful IT transformation is more about leadership than it is about IT. We discovered that successful transformational leaders take their leadership responsibilities seriously, and they hone their leadership skills to a fine edge.

We also discovered that successful transformational leaders spend a lot of time listening and communicating. They focus on developing empathy and understanding. They assume that business leaders will not be able to express their needs in terms that translate easily into IT requirements, so they don't become frustrated by vague or nonspecific requests.

Lesson

Leading a successful IT transformation is more about leadership than it is about IT. Successful transformational leaders take their leadership responsibilities seriously, and they hone their leadership skills to a fine edge.

Most of all, they realize that IT leadership is an ongoing process of relationship building and relationship management, a process of continuous involvement and engagement with other leaders across the enterprise.

Harry Pickett is the global CTO at Manulife Financial, a large Canadian-based financial services company operating in 22 countries and territories worldwide. Its best-known U.S. subsidiary is John Hancock. We met with Harry in Toronto, and then spoke with him again by phone. We asked Harry to describe the challenges of IT leadership in a turbulent, rapidly shifting economy. Here are the highlights of our conversations:

Business leaders generally describe their business goals in very high-level terms. For example, they might say, "We need to double our revenue in the next five years." And if someone asks them to outline the strategy that will accomplish this goal, they might say, "We plan to accomplish our goals through a combination of organic growth of existing products, the introduction of new products and services, and key acquisitions to grow market share."

In a high-level business conversation, all of that sounds perfectly reasonable. But it doesn't mean a heck of a lot to IT.

Lesson

Transformational leaders spend a lot of time listening and communicating. They focus on developing empathy and understanding. They assume that business leaders will not be able to express their needs in terms that translate easily into IT requirements, so they don't become frustrated by vague or nonspecific requests.

In the past, IT would have pushed back with a lot of questions, such as, "When you say 'organic growth,' what precisely do you mean?" or "How exactly will the new services be offered?" or "Have you considered the time and cost required to integrate the IT systems of the acquired companies?"

Then IT would gather lists of business requirements, translate them into system requirements, create system definitions based on the requirements, present the definitions to the business and ask, "Is this what you were talking about?" That traditional process for developing new systems has "changed radically," says Harry.

Today, IT is more likely to listen to the business, visualize the challenges in technical terms, outline the options for accomplishing the business goals, and then work collaboratively with the business leaders to deploy the solutions that make the most sense for the company.

The business will never just say, "Here's our strategy, now go away and make it happen." What you'll have is an interactive process in which IT works with the business to achieve the

"Business leaders generally describe their business goals in very high-level terms. For example, they might say, 'We need to double our revenue in the next five years.' . . . In a high-level business conversation . . . that sounds perfectly reasonable. But it doesn't mean a heck of a lot to IT."

desired goals. The challenge for IT is describing the solution in terms that the business will truly understand and embrace.

Business leaders have very little patience for technobabble; their eyes glaze over. Good IT people know how to describe solutions in real business language. Does this mean that IT is bending a little bit more than it did in the past? Yes, but that's part of the job today.

When IT proposes a new initiative, the proposal is composed in plain language that addresses a business challenge, says Harry.

In the past, we might have said, "We want to buy this new computer because it's state of the art, it's faster, it's more efficient." Today, we would say, "This newer technology will improve your cycle times and provide you with the critical information you need more quickly and in a format that is easier to interpret." Or we might say, "We can help you reduce your product development costs and get your new products to market faster and ahead of the competition."

Or we might put it this way: "Given that you want to double your business in five years, we'll need to spend $10 million on *application modernization because you won't be able to grow at a fast pace with 10 systems doing things 10 different ways. We'll need to get down to two or three systems to achieve the kind of efficiency you'll need to achieve your business goals."*

Today's IT leaders have to make presentations that stay resolutely focused on business needs, with as little focus on technology as possible.

Obviously, you're going to have an appendix slide showing them a picture of the new system you're talking about. And fortunately, many business people are more savvy about technology than they were in the past; they're more interested and they're less intimidated. But if you start off by saying, "This will be a Parallel Sysplex operation with high availability and we're going to load-balance your servers and both your Web application and your database," then all of a sudden you've lost them.

It's better to say something like, "Basically, we're going to create an environment that allows you to fail over. If your primary system drops down, we'll use your development system, and that will improve your cost ratio. The only downside is that your development system will be out of the water for a couple of hours until we have the primary back up." Now you've said the same thing, but you've put it in words that have meaning for the business.

Another challenge for IT leaders, especially in large organizations that have grown through multiple acquisitions and mergers, is promoting the adoption of standard processes— while respecting the independence of the individual divisions and units within the enterprise.

> "We might put it this way: 'Given that you want
> to double your business in five years, we'll need
> to spend $10 million on application moderniza-
> tion because you won't be able to grow at a fast
> pace with 10 systems doing things 10 different
> ways. We'll need to get down to two or three
> systems to achieve the kind of efficiency you'll
> need to achieve your business goals.'"

At large companies with multiple operating units and decentralized command structures, it's not uncommon for different units to launch their own versions of the same IT project. Harry says that one of his goals is finding ways for the business units to share projects and avoid unnecessary duplication of effort.

"What we do instead is identify common elements in the projects," says Harry. "Then we explain to the business units that it makes better sense to create one version of the solution and share it across four units than it does to develop four different versions of the same solution."

Harry and his team work with subject matter experts (SMEs) from the business units to ensure that everyone is happy with the end results of their shared efforts. "We have 2,500 people in IT and we're trying to tap into the intellectual capital of those people, while honoring the federated nature of the company. We've created what we call 'standard work groups' to focus on developing common solutions that everybody needs. But that doesn't stop the units from developing unique projects on their own. We just want to make sure that we're not creating four or five different solutions to solve the same business problem."

Best of Both Worlds

In a very real sense, Harry is trying to blend the power and clout of a highly centralized organization with the speed and agility of a looser, more decentralized organization. It's a balancing act, to be sure, but one that Harry enjoys performing.

> *This is the best job I've ever had. I've done application development, I've run infrastructure, I've set up networks, and I've managed service operations. Because of my range of experience, I've developed a broader, more horizontal view of the enterprise.*
>
> *It's still not unusual to find people who've spent 30 years in the network division, or 20 years in applications testing. But it's harder to make good decisions if you view everything from the perspective of your own little technology silo. If you want to be a good IT leader who makes good decisions, it helps to be a generalist.*

Sourcing is an area in which the ability to make the right decisions consistently can create or destroy a competitive advantage. "One thing we've discovered is that it's important to let other people do some of the work for you," says Harry. "For example, we're carving off blocks of our application development. We have managed services in our infrastructure environments. We pay other companies to run our data center operations so we don't have to spend huge amounts of capital building new data centers."

While some functions can be outsourced with minimal risks, other functions must be kept closer to home. "We're looking at which business processes we can move offshore, and which we want to retain. Over time, we are reengineering IT and creating a whole new way of delivering systems. It's futuristic, and we're pretty excited about the possibilities."

IT Thought Leadership

Another interesting topic that surfaced during my conversation with Harry was thought leadership. When we asked him about the proper role of IT in providing thought leadership for the rest of the company, he quickly noted that while "IT does not have a monopoly on thought leadership," it is uniquely positioned to offer guidance, particularly at the business unit level.

"We're not a bleeding-edge technology company. We're pretty conservative," says Harry. "But at the same time, we need to understand the potential impact of new technologies on our business. Part of my role as global CTO is looking around, seeing what's happening in our industry and imagining the future—before it happens. That's one of the ways we stay competitive."

Imagining, anticipating, and preparing for the future helps the company do the best possible job of placing its bets on the right technology investments. In difficult economic times,

" . . . we need to understand the potential impact of new technologies on our business. Part of my role as global CTO is looking around, seeing what's happening in our industry and imagining the future—before it happens. That's one of the ways we stay competitive."

such as now, directing investment capital toward projects that will generate the highest returns is no trivial matter. IT's ability to function as a clearinghouse for new technology projects makes it an invaluable resource to the enterprise.

Traditionally, each business unit had to prove that it could afford the cost of any new project that it proposed. The downside of the traditional approach is that individual business units often refrain from seeking newer technologies that might help them become more competitive and more profitable.

Today, for example, Harry's team might make the business case for acquiring a newer technology and offering it as a shared service across the enterprise.

"As a global organization, we can gather requirements across many lines of business and make the case for a foundational investment that helps multiple lines of business move their agendas forward," Harry explains. "That's part of the role we play as thought leaders. We try to determine which

"As a global organization, we can gather requirements across many lines of business
and make the case for a foundational investment that helps multiple lines of business
move their agendas forward. That's part of
the role we play as thought leaders. We try to
determine which technology investments will
drive the highest value for the company, and
then we figure out how to make those investments affordable."

technology investments will drive the highest value for the
company, and then we figure out how to make those investments affordable."

From my perspective, this strategic-level approach to technology investment—whether you call it "thought leadership"
or "globally shared technology services"—represents the real
future of IT in the modern enterprise.

A Magical Decision

When Walt Disney Parks and Resorts asked Roger Berry to
become its next CIO, the post reported to the division's CFO.
Roger told the Disney folks that he would consider their
offer—but only if the CIO reported directly to the division's
president.

Disney agreed to Roger's request. The decision turned out
to be a great one for both Roger and the division. Soon after

Roger's arrival, the division unveiled a new strategy for building better, deeper, and more profitable relationships with its guests. The new strategy was called "Magic Your Way," and it represented a truly dramatic leap forward.

But the new strategy had a serious flaw—the existing IT infrastructure could not support it. Here's how Roger recalls the moment he realized that he was in deep water:

> *I remember the first big meeting on Magic Your Way. I came in and sat down with the president and the CFO. They were going through what they wanted to do, and they'd done some preliminary work before I arrived about the cost. I listened to all of it, and I realized there wasn't anything about infrastructure and technology in the plan.*
>
> *So I raised my hand . . . I was new there . . . I said, "Time out." I said, "Do you realize that what you're trying to do is put an elephant on a Tonka toy? It's not going to work. Your infrastructure can't carry that kind of load."*
>
> *Immediately—it was the first real test for me—I said, "You're going to have to change your whole model around how you're going to fund this thing. You've got a lot bigger investment to make in technology than your plan shows." They already had it laid out for five years of what they wanted to do, but they didn't have the technology piece of it.*
>
> *One of the many things that I admire about Disney is this: When they come up with a good idea, they will stay with that idea until they figure it out. I've worked with a lot of companies where you can come up with a great idea, but then the finance guys look at it and say, "Oh, we can't afford it," and the idea gets trashed.*

Disney doesn't do that. When they have an idea that they truly believe will enhance their services or their product or will give them a competitive advantage, they will stay with that idea and iterate on it until they figure out how to do it. Even if the technology is not there to deliver it, they will hold that idea until the technology evolves and then deploy it. That is a real strength of Disney.

Roger's willingness to stand up in front of the business equivalent of a moving freight train earned him the trust and respect of the division's senior management team. But it didn't magically solve the multiple challenges that are inherent in any large-scale transformation effort.

As it turned out, the division's IT infrastructure was only one dimension of the problem. "We could upgrade the infrastructure," says Roger. "What proved more difficult was getting the people in IT to focus on new ways of doing things."

In the past, the IT organization had focused most of its bandwidth on maintaining the division's aging IT assets. Roger quickly understood that one of his primary leadership tasks would be shifting the IT organization's focus. Essentially, he would have to transform IT from a high-tech maintenance department into a highly motivated team that focused on supporting innovation.

To accomplish this organizational transformation with minimal disruption and maximum efficiency, Roger employed a practical leadership strategy with three interrelated and mutually reinforcing components. I like Roger's approach to transformational leadership because it's simple, and at the same time comprehensive. Best of all, it proved effective in a situation that could have easily spun out of control.

Here is an ultracondensed version of the leadership strategy that worked for Roger at Disney:

1. *All-In Partnership.* Engage the executives; align from top down and bottom up; establish clear communication; listen and take action; inspire trust ("I've got your back").

2. *People Power.* Align IT with the heart of the business; establish emotional connection with transformation strategy; prioritize (company first, team second, individual last); empower the team; "walk the talk"; reinforce and reward courageous behavior.

3. *Surprise Management.* Establish critical risk criteria; raise the alarm the instant something goes wrong; have a clear escalation/mobilization process; identify potential problems before they occur; maintain a 24/7 sense of urgency; keep top executives informed.

Roger's strategy set the stage for a spectacular period of growth at the parks and resorts division. The close bond between IT and the business resulted in what Roger describes as a "cycle of continuous innovation" that helped Disney maintain its leadership position in an increasingly competitive industry.

> ## Lesson
>
> If Roger hadn't raised his hand, if he hadn't had the courage and the skill to explain the underlying reality of the situation, the company's visionary strategy would surely have been delayed or possibly even derailed.

"Put Yourself in the CEO's Shoes"

The story of Roger's willingness to confront his new bosses is both instructive and inspirational. If Roger hadn't raised his hand, if he hadn't had the courage and the skill to explain the underlying reality of the situation, the company's visionary strategy would surely have been delayed or possibly even derailed.

This brings me to another point about IT leadership: It's not something that can be taken for granted or treated lightly. IT leadership is like any other form of executive leadership: it requires a combination of confidence, knowledge, empathy, strength, and courage. You can't just show up and wing it—you have to be ready to engage and to play the game at the executive level.

Perry Rotella is the CIO at Verisk Analytics, a company based in Jersey City, New Jersey, that provides information and analytic tools to help customers manage risk. Like most of the CIOs I've met, Perry is a smart guy, and a practical realist. When I asked Perry to name a critical skill that you learn on the job, he replied immediately with one word: leadership.

Lesson

IT leadership is like any other form of executive leadership: It requires a combination of confidence, knowledge, empathy, strength, and courage.

"At the executive level, it's all about leadership," says Perry. "I have found that if you take responsibility, if you take initiative, if you take ownership—then you can really drive solutions and guide people toward doing great things. It doesn't matter that you run the most efficient data center or complete development projects successfully. What matters is consistently helping the company transform itself to be the best it can be."

A key part of executive leadership, says Perry, is establishing a sense of urgency. "Even if there's not a burning platform, you need to help people overcome their inertia. You need to help them grasp the importance of what they're doing. You need to be the person who lights fires under people and gets them going. That's a critical part of your role as a leader."

Part of Perry's ability to motivate people comes from his experience as a consultant. Here's how he explains it:

I spent the first 14 years of my career at a consulting firm. We specialized in systems integration, but we were always looking for ways to help our clients grow their businesses. We were very aware of the business implications of what we were doing.

When you're a consultant, a lot of what you're really doing is business transformation. That's because companies bring

> "I have found that if you take responsibility, if you take initiative, if you take ownership—then you can really drive solutions and guide people toward doing great things. It doesn't matter that you run the most efficient data center or complete development projects successfully. What matters is consistently helping the company transform itself to be the best it can be."

you in to get things done that they can't do on their own. At the same time, however, you have no real authority or status within the company that hires you. So you have to learn how to lead and how to influence people even when you have no direct authority.

One sure way to establish your credibility as a consultant is always remembering why you were hired, says Perry.

When you're sitting with a client, whatever you're discussing, your role as a consultant is helping the client achieve their business objectives. I bring that same mind-set to my role as CIO. You have to be able to step outside your comfort zone and remember that your real job is helping the business increase shareholder value. You have to put yourself in the CEO's shoes.

Perry says that he learned to focus on results as a young football player in Danbury, Connecticut. "I wasn't the biggest or the fastest kid, but I worked hard on the field and I wasn't easily intimidated. You need that kind of attitude to be a successful CIO."

Lesson

A key part of executive leadership is establishing a sense of urgency. "Even if there's not a burning platform, you need to help people overcome their inertia."

Confronting Reality

Being an executive leader is not easy, and it is not always intuitive. You have to be willing to take some hard knocks, pick yourself up off the floor, and return to the battle. You must not only demand respect from your peers, you must earn it— over and over.

Mark P. McDonald, the group vice president of executive programs at Gartner, is a terrific speaker. I had the privilege of listening to one of his presentations at the CIO Executive Leadership Roundtable in Chicago recently. Mark also writes an excellent blog. One of his posts is titled "General support means no support," and it describes in somewhat horrifying detail an executive-level meeting in which the CIO of a company presents his vision and strategy for the next three years.

After the CIO concludes his presentation, the CFO asks the CIO if there's anything specific that he needs to achieve his plan. CIO responds by saying that he needs the CFO's "sponsorship." The CIO does not specify what he needs from the leadership team; instead he merely seeks their general support. Here are snippets from Mark's post:

I almost fell out of my chair. . . . The CFO who had been engaged in the conversation visibly sat back in his chair and disengaged. . . . It became blindingly clear: General support means no support.

Unwittingly, the CIO has missed a "tremendous opportunity" to gather the concrete support and executive engagement that he will need to move forward with his proposed strategy, Mark writes.

It is a weakness to ask for general help. It is a strength to know what you need, why you need it and to ask. Recognize that when you say that you need this person to do that, you are demonstrating your knowledge and mastery of the challenges ahead . . . When you don't ask for specific support, you tell your peers that the project does not really matter.

Mark's blog entry really hit the bull's-eye. How many of us find it difficult to ask for the things we really need to succeed? How many of us fall back on platitudes that later prove to be meaningless? How many of us do our homework so that when we're confronted with difficult questions, we can reply with honest, accurate answers?

It's not easy to look in the mirror and say, "You know, I need to do a better job of communicating, and I need to improve the way I relate to my executive peers." But sometimes that is exactly what we need to do: Take a good, long look in the mirror and ask ourselves if we're being thoroughly, totally honest.

"When you don't ask for specific support, you tell your peers that the project does not really matter."

No Illusions

Roberta Kowalishin is the CIO at the *Houston Chronicle*, the nation's seventh-largest daily paper and the leader in Web technology across Hearst Newspapers. The *Chronicle*'s web site, chron.com, is regarded as one of the top newspaper web sites, receiving more than 75 million page views on average per month.

Like the home mortgage industry and the domestic automobile industry, the newspaper industry has suffered through hard times. Readership and ad revenues have dwindled steadily for years. Dozens of newspapers have already folded; the surviving newspapers face an uncertain future.

The *Chronicle*'s parent company, Hearst Corporation, owns a chain of 15 newspapers. Hearst plans to consolidate the chain's IT services into a unified organization run by a global CIO. Roberta has been tapped for the job, and she harbors few illusions about the difficulties ahead.

We caught up with her recently, and asked her to describe the qualities required to succeed as an IT leader in today's turbulent economy.

"The qualities of good leadership haven't changed over the years. You still have to set the vision and then help the team achieve that vision," says Roberta. "But what's really different is the time window and the need to deliver results very quickly. We used to make a three-year or a five-year plan. Today, everything changes so rapidly, you don't know what's going to happen next. Everything happens much more quickly. You're forced to make decisions faster. It can be exhausting."

When business conditions change so rapidly and so dramatically, the very concept of "vision" can seem outdated. "Some employees are uncomfortable working without a clear vision and strategy, but in many cases today, we are experimenting and innovating and don't always have a single vision or direction. This is a big change from the slower-paced environments of the past, where a business had time to reflect and communicate a single vision or strategy. It is challenging to function without the vision," says Roberta. "They need answers. . . . But we don't always know the answers."

In many instances, the answers are not comforting. When changing market conditions force companies to downsize, there are no easy remedies, no painless solutions. While it might be tempting to assign blame or to look for scapegoats, it would also be futile and counterproductive. "It's nobody's fault when your company has to shrink because the market isn't buying your products or services," says Roberta. "That's just the way it is."

Lesson

When changing market conditions force companies to downsize, there are no easy remedies, no painless solutions. While it might be tempting to assign blame or to look for scapegoats, it would also be futile and counterproductive.

Roberta says that she has learned to adapt to this kind of accelerated and highly uncertain environment and she looks to recruit people with the ability to live and add value in the present and enjoy the ambiguity and evolving nature of the business climate. This new environment does pose challenges for colleagues who struggle with change; in a sense, they are still living in the past—a past in which every question had an answer and time itself seemed to flow at a more leisurely pace.

For Roberta and other IT executives in struggling parts of the economy, leadership isn't about flowery words and abstract management jargon—it's about getting the job done at the lowest cost and with the fewest people.

"Most of the significant changes we can make in technology will affect people—especially where external service providers can provide services at lower cost than our internal teams. Even though our employees know that our industry is seeing dramatic declines in revenue, attitudes and behaviors on the team can still reflect the expectation that was common

Lesson

Guiding organizational change is another critical facet of IT leadership. In addition to mastering technology and finance, a successful IT leader must also master the art of change management.

several decades ago, where employees could expect a company to take care of them for life. But that's not the reality anymore, and part of my job is to help our team understand a changing vision based on this reality."

After listening to Roberta's story, I realized that guiding organizational change is another critical facet of IT leadership. In addition to mastering technology and finance, a successful IT leader must also master the art of change management.

Which brings us neatly to another key point: In most situations, people are reluctant to change. Resisting change is human nature; but it's also a management challenge. That means that the transformational CIO must be adept at convincing people that there are compelling reasons for adapting to change, accepting change, and embracing change—even when change results in discomfort and dislocation.

It's hard work convincing people that change is necessary and good—but it's a key part of the CIO's role as master of change management, and there's no way around that fact. Either you convince people that change is good, or you convince them to work somewhere else.

Lesson

It's hard work convincing people that change is necessary and good—but it's a key part of the CIO's role, and there's no way around that fact. Either you convince people that change is good, or you convince them to work somewhere else.

Chapter 5

Mapping *Your* Future

Executive Summary

If you really want to know what's going on in the world of corporate IT, ask an executive recruiter. If you really want to know which career strategies are effective—and which are not—you can find out by talking to an executive recruiter. The folks in this chapter have placed many of the CIOs working today at top companies all over the world. They offer some great advice, and I sincerely hope that you pick up a helpful nugget or two from the pages that follow.

I have always made it a priority to invite the *crème de la crème* of executive recruiters to my CIO events, and as a result, I have built a sturdy network of experts upon whom I can rely for highly precise, up-to-the-minute knowledge about the state of IT executive leadership.

Time after time, the insight of these executive recruiters has proven invaluable to me. That's why the first chapter of this book focuses on their observations and perspectives on the rapidly changing universe of executive IT leadership.

Most of the critical knowledge contained in this chapter has been gleaned from a series of exclusive, in-depth interviews conducted with top executive recruiters at leading global search firms. I have personally known most of these executive recruiters for many years, and I truly value their collective wisdom.

After all, they are paid to ignore the hype and self-promotion that tends to shroud the truth about many organizations. It's almost as if they have some kind of X-ray vision enabling them to strip away the nonsense and get right to the core. To be honest, sometimes their ability to discern the signal through all the noise is downright scary!

I have known many executive recruiters over the years, and I consider several of them to be close friends. I can tell you honestly that what excites them the most is finding the right person for the right open post at the right company. That requires lots of deep drilling over a wide area. They study the company and they study the pool of available talent. Their job is recommending candidates who will succeed in executive posts at major corporations, where the expectations will be astronomically high and the demands will be absolutely excruciating.

While some executive recruiters might find the term "head-hunter" vaguely flattering, the truth is that most of them see themselves as highly specialized knowledge workers.

So let's pick their brains for some of the crucial knowledge you will need to move forward in your career and achieve your goals. You might not agree with everything they say, but I guarantee that you will find their observations useful and interesting.

What I *Really* Want Is a Business Partner . . .

My friend Mark Polansky leads the CIO practice at Korn/Ferry International. He's been keeping a close eye on the industry for a very long time, and I respect his opinions greatly.

I asked him recently to list the qualities that CEOs and executive boards look for in a new CIO. Here's what he told me:

Well, the conversation turns really quickly to leadership, because leadership is what separates great executives from ordinary executives. They also look for vision, passion, wisdom, confidence, and charisma.

Clients often tell Mark that they are looking for someone who is persuasive without being overbearing, knows when to take risks (and when not to), and is creative but also realistic, supportive but firm, principled, honest, fair, and open. Very few clients mention specific technical knowledge or expertise.

"All things being equal, someone with a strong technical background is likely to be more successful, but I think what's equally important is the ability to attract top performers. In other words, the CIO has to be a talent magnet," says Mark.

James Satterthwaite of Egon Zehnder International put it this way at a recent CIO Roundtable hosted by my company, HMG Strategy, and the Boston chapter of the Society of Information Managers (SIM):

The board members sense that the CIO position is more important than ever, but they can't always put their feelings into words. Often they'll say that they're looking for a business partner. What I think they really mean is that they're looking for a leader, someone with passion who can help them make the company really great . . .

Shawn Banerji of Russell Reynolds Associates specializes in recruiting CIOs for major corporations. He affirms the idea that when companies look for senior technology executives, they're looking for business leaders.

First and foremost, a great CIO is also a great business person. It really begins and ends with that. Yes, you need to be a competent technologist, but if you don't have the business skills, it's going to be very difficult to succeed in today's environment.

A great CIO creates a vision of IT that reflects his or her understanding of the marketplace and anticipates change so that IT can be leveraged as a vehicle for creating competitive advantages. That is becoming more critical as technology permeates every aspect of every business.

At the same time, a great CIO needs to be strong on execution. That means the CIO has to be a tremendous program manager and be capable of keeping business objectives in mind while making important decisions about allocating resources and capital.

And all of that requires strong financial skills and superior business judgment so the CIO can set goals, meet deadlines, and stay on budget.

> "A great CIO creates a vision of IT that reflects his or her understanding of the marketplace and anticipates change so that IT can be leveraged as a vehicle for creating competitive advantages."

Tarun Inuganti, who recruits technology executives at Spencer Stuart, puts superior communications skills near the top of his list of key attributes required to lead modern IT departments.

When you are the CIO, your most critical skill is your ability to communicate your message at all the different levels and functional areas of the organization. Each audience has a different way of listening and communicating. Great CIOs adapt their communication styles to match the audience they're interacting with.

If you are the CIO of a large global enterprise, you might be meeting with the managers of a $3 billion business one day and the managers of a $30 billion business the next day. You have to communicate your message equally well to both audiences. That requires special leadership skill.

Katie Graham and Bryan MacDonald are top recruiters at Heidrick & Struggles, a global executive search and leadership consulting firm. They agree that communication skills can make or break a CIO.

"In many cases, the CEO expresses frustration over communications between IT and the business. The CEO wants a CIO who really understands the business and who can deliver effective solutions without all the tech talk," says Katie.

Bryan concurs, but adds a warning:

Many CIOs seem to suggest they are aware of this macro issue. But, at the same time, most think that they're personally doing a good job of communicating with the executive team and

> "CIOs need to become much more self-aware. I would advise them to poll their past and present customers, and ask them to honestly evaluate the quality of their relationship with them as a leader. Ask them what worked, what didn't work."

bridging the gap between IT and its customers, when the reality is, there are still a number of examples of severe disconnect.

CIOs need to become much more self-aware. I would advise them to poll their past and present customers and ask them to honestly evaluate the quality of their relationship with them as a leader. Ask them what worked, what didn't work. Ask them for suggestions for improving the relationship between IT and the business. Most of all, ask them for some honest advice. They'll hear some interesting things, for sure.

Katie suggests using executive recruiters who specialize in IT placements as sounding boards. "Sometimes just talking to us can be useful. We're happy to give you feedback and advice," says Katie. "I think it's also a good way to build a trusting relationship. That way, when you're ready to make a move, you're not picking up the phone and calling someone you don't already know. From my perspective, I'd say that 80 percent of the placements I make involve people I've known over time and already trust."

Get Yourself a Business Mentor *and* a Coach

Everyone needs and deserves a business mentor. A business mentor is usually someone else in your organization. Usually a mentor is a peer or someone at a higher level than you. If you are the CIO, your business mentor can be the CEO or another senior executive.

Basically the role of your business mentor is to answer questions that you have about the business. The questions can range from basic ("What's a basis point, anyhow?") to complex ("How does the company book revenue from sales made by foreign subsidiaries?").

Business mentors can also help you avoid nasty political landmines and steer clear of time-wasting intramural feuds. Most of all, a business mentor can offer real-time situational advice that no outside expert can provide.

If you can't find an appropriate mentor within your organization, ask someone you respect to serve in the role.

Some of the smartest executives I know sought out personal coaches to tutor them as they transitioned through the multiple stages of their careers. I believe that hiring a coach is one of the savviest career decisions you can make.

A coach can help you acquire and sharpen the crucial executive skills you need to succeed at the C-level. While it's true that some fortunate individuals are born with the talents required to function at the highest corporate levels, the sad truth is that most of us have to learn them.

How do you find an executive coach? Ask your friends. Ask the head of HR. Ask your business mentor. Or send me an e-mail at hunterm@hmgstrategy.com, and I'll try to connect you with the resources you need to find the right one.

Do I Really Need an MBA?

Well, no. But it certainly helps. Many of the CIOs you will read about in the subsequent pages of this book have MBAs. One or two have law degrees. Some have advanced degrees in computer science, but increasingly they are the exception.

If you ask the executive recruiters quoted earlier to tell you what qualities they look for in a CIO, all of their answers would sound something like this:

The qualities we look for in a CIO are the exact same qualities we look for in any C-level executive.

The modern CIO is expected to be a well-rounded, well-educated, and highly sophisticated senior business executive who can represent the organization credibly and honorably in any sort of milieu, whether it's an investor conference or a charity ball.

Great CIOs prepare themselves by reading books on a multitude of subjects, by serving on various company committees, by participating in community activities, by joining local

"The qualities we look for in a CIO are the exact same qualities we look for in any C-level executive."

clubs and teams, by volunteering for international assign-ments, by rotating through different functional areas of the company, by taking advanced business courses, by writing books, articles, and blogs . . .

Does this sound like the description of a Renaissance man or Renaissance woman? Is there something wrong with the idea that the CIO should be more than just some kind of ele-vated technocrat?

Your Seat at the Table Is Waiting

It seems like every book written about the CIO in the past 10 years has included the phrase "a seat at the table." CIOs were reminded constantly that unless they managed to secure "a seat at the table," they would face inevitable doom.

When you hear the phrase nowadays, it's likely to be spoken with a certain degree of irony. Most new CIOs are expected to sit at the executive table—and they are also expected to perform at the same level as their exec-utive peers.

Think about this for a moment: Back in the good old days, the CIO could hide behind a wall of technology. IT was a mysterious "black box," and when it didn't work as adver-tised or failed to deliver real value, people weren't really sur-prised or terribly disappointed.

Those days are gone. People expect technology to work and to deliver real value. When it doesn't, they hold the CIO responsible. Suddenly that "seat at the table" doesn't feel so comfortable anymore.

My friend Beverly Lieberman is president of Halbrecht Lieberman Associates in Westport, Connecticut. HLA is a "boutique" executive search firm specializing in senior-level IT placements. Over the past three years, Beverly says, there's been a real change in the way that CIOs are perceived by the board and by other C-level executives.

"Now the CIO is expected to be an executive leader with visibility and clout throughout the company," says Beverly. "Many CIOs already sit on executive committees on a peer level with the heads of marketing, sales, operations and finance. They've made it to the cabinet, and they are expected to operate at the highest levels of executive leadership."

Until fairly recently, the typical CIO reported to the CFO or COO. Unless there was an emergency, the CIO rarely met with the company's executive board. Despite the "C" in his or her title, the CIO was still viewed as the manager of a back office service function.

Transformational CIOs report directly to their CEOs or COOs. That puts them front and center when critical decisions affecting the business are made. Now the stakes are much higher. Most of the conversations taking place around the executive table don't focus on operational details—they focus on business strategy. For many CIOs, executive meetings can be rude awakenings.

Lesson

Transformational CIOs report directly to their CEOs or COOs. That puts them front and center when critical decisions affecting the business are made.

"Until three or four years ago, there weren't many business-oriented CIOs," says Beverly. "Most CIOs were technology oriented. And many tended to be introverts, which made it harder for them to develop the kind of relationships required for success at the executive level."

But the tide seems to be turning. Compared to their predecessors, today's CIOs seem generally more aware of business concepts, and today's CEOs seem generally more appreciative of technology. The more common ground they share, the more likely they are to trust each other.

"Most CEOs come from sales, marketing, or finance. So it's not surprising that they feel higher levels of synergy and comfort with executives who have had similar experiences," observes Beverly. "The relationship between the CEO and the CIO is just beginning to jell, and it's still evolving."

As greater numbers of tech-savvy executives are promoted to the corner office, it seems logical to assume that working relationships between CEOs and their CIOs will become much closer and more productive.

"A CEO who grew up with technology will be much more inclined to embrace the CIO as a business partner and a confidante," says Beverly.

Are You Sowing Seeds for Success— or Failure?

From my perspective, Beverly's observations are spot on. Newer CEOs seem to understand intuitively that technology plays a huge role in determining the success or failure of their tenure at the helm. It makes sense that these newer CEOs will increasingly rely on their CIOs to serve as trusted advisors and key players on executive teams.

At the same time, it seems fairly obvious that even when a CEO does not share an affinity for technology with the CIO, the CEO still counts on the CIO to succeed—after all, that's why the CIO was hired.

All of this seems to be good news for CIOs. But it also raises an interesting question: *Why* do CIOs often fail? In many instances, it seems that a CIO's success or failure depends far less on technical competency than on social competency.

In Chapter 4, we looked at some of the leadership skills required to stay afloat in the executive ocean. And in Chapter 6, we look at what you need to accomplish in your first 30 days on the job.

But we thought it would be a good idea to check in now with Tony Leng, a managing partner at Hodge Partners, an executive search firm based in San Francisco and Atlanta. We asked him to tell us what his priorities would be if he was a newly hired CIO.

"If you're a new CIO, the first thing you've got to do is get out there and start talking to your internal customers. You can't sit quietly behind your desk waiting for people to come to you with their problems. That is the worst possible strategy. You must spend time in the trenches with your internal customers, listening to them and learning from them," says Tony. "You must understand their pain so you can help them."

The next crucial action step for a new CIO is meeting and talking with the company's external customers. "You've got to find out what they're thinking about your company. Is there an issue with the interface? If there is, can the issue be resolved through technology? Or is it a process issue, or a people issue? Or a combination? You can find out by talking directly with the external customers."

Once you've got a handle on the issues that are riling up your customers, both internally and externally, you can move swiftly to accomplish your first do-or-die mission as CIO: establishing your credibility as an executive.

"Look around, find something that's broken and fix it. Look for something that the other executives really want, something that the previous CIO didn't deliver. And then deliver it," advises Tony. "It doesn't have to be something big, it can be a small project. What's important is getting it done right and getting it done quickly."

Focus on creating a short-term gain by driving cost or complexity out of the organization. Better still, find projects that will add business value by tapping into new revenue streams or accelerating the launch of a new product.

"You are the CIO—the person who sees all of the company's processes and all of the company's data. You should be able to say, 'Look, here are some new products or new markets or new tactics we can use to make more money for the company.' That's what the CEO and the other executives need to hear from you," says Tony.

Even if you've been hired to solve a major problem, such as a stalled ERP implementation or the rollout of a new manufacturing system, it still makes sense to seize opportunities for quick wins that will build confidence.

One example that springs to mind involves a CIO who was brought in to manage the implementation of an enterprise financial intelligence platform at a major insurance company.

Even though the new CIO knew that his primary duty was rolling out the new platform, he also knew that he had to establish his credibility and the credibility of his team. Being a smart CIO, he met with his internal customers and quickly discovered that many of them had difficulty communicating with their IT managers.

As it happened, the fix was relatively simple: He reassigned managers from the central IT office to the company's various operating units, where they could work directly with their internal customers. And he told the IT managers that from that point forward, their performance reviews would be based on their ability to keep their internal customers happy.

I love that story, because it illustrates how a business-savvy CIO can achieve a quick victory without spending tons of money. Basically, he rearranged desks—and it worked brilliantly.

Of course, he still has to succeed with his primary assignment of rolling out the new finance platform. But his early win created the breathing room—and the good will—that he will need to achieve his main objective.

And this brings us neatly to another important point: Something will always go wrong . . .

Managing Expectations

A CIO at a major global bank once told me that his colleagues often criticized him for "turning every request into a project." While I can sympathize with the frustration of his colleagues, I can also understand his point of view.

After you've been in the IT business for a while, you know there are no simple solutions. Everything you do in IT involves varying degrees of complexity. And that means that sooner or later something will break, or not work as it was supposed to work, or disappoint someone who expected one kind of result and instead got something else.

Extremely complex projects—and almost all business transformation projects qualify as "extremely complex"—have thousands of moving parts. Each of those parts can potentially fail. Rest assured that some of them will.

If you have committed the time and the effort required to build good working relationships with the CEO and your executive peers, you will be in a far better position to weather the storm when things break.

The credibility and trust you have established in your first weeks and months on the job will be needed when the network goes down, the sales force is locked out of the CRM system, the data warehouse crashes, or the e-mail suddenly stops working.

Most important, if you have been hired to lead a business transformation project, your ability to inspire trust and confidence will be tested time and time again, because transformation projects often take years to complete.

So it is absolutely imperative that you resist the urge to sugarcoat problems or gloss over potential obstacles. Remember, one of the first rules of management is NO SURPRISES.

"A lot of CIOs have gotten into trouble because they didn't adequately prepare the executive team for all of the problems that inevitably occur during a business transformation project," says Beverly. "They tend to undermanage expectations, which is always a big mistake. Because when things go wrong and the senior executives are pulling out their hair, they assume that the CIO doesn't know what he or she is doing. In most cases, the CIO does know what to do and is doing the right thing. The real problem, however, is that the CIO has not prepared the other executives for all of the possible pitfalls."

When the CIO is forthrightly honest and candid about everything that can possibly go wrong, it's much harder for other executives to claim they were surprised when things *do* go wrong.

> ## Lesson
>
> If you have been hired to lead a business transformation project, your ability to inspire trust and confidence will be tested time and time again, because transformation projects often take years to complete.

Chapter 6

The First 30 Days

Executive Summary

As the saying goes, you only have one chance to make a good first impression. Remember that nobody really cares about technology—they care about what technology can do for them. Listen carefully to your new colleagues, figure out what they need, and then try to deliver solutions that address their needs. You can't change the world in 30 days, but you can find quick wins that will demonstrate your abilities and your understanding of the business.

B ack in 2003, Michael Watkins wrote *The First 90 Days*. It's a great book, and most of the successful senior executives I know have a copy of it tucked away on a bookshelf.

For better or worse, people begin judging a new CIO immediately—there is no honeymoon, no grace period. You walk in the door and people expect you to perform miracles. It's all part of the IT mystique—the curse and the blessing of modern technology.

When you're the CIO, you're living in an accelerated universe. Everybody wants something from you *now*. So you need to be prepared, you need to be ready, and you need to know what you're going to do *before you walk in the door*.

That's the reality of being the CIO in today's hypercompetitive economy.

Let Everyone Know That You're Organized

Mike Pellegrino is the CIO at Frontier Communications Corporation. Frontier's corporate headquarters are in Stamford, Connecticut, but the company serves customers in 27 states and is the largest provider of communications services to rural America.

Mike arrived at the company during a period of transition, which is not in itself surprising—it's fairly common practice for companies to hire new CIOs at the beginning of transitional periods. Hiring a new CIO is one way for senior management to send a clear message to everyone that change is in the air.

What is uncommon, however, is the degree to which Mike was ready for his new role. If it seemed to the folks at Frontier that Mike hit the ground running, it was because he began preparing long before he even got the job. Here's a summary of Mike's process, in his own words:

> *When you're interviewing, you have to assume that you're going to get the job. During the interview process, which typically goes four or five rounds, you're going to meet with lots of people. So you'll have plenty of opportunities to ask questions about the business. They think they're interviewing you, but the truth is that you're interviewing them. Use what you learn during the interviews to set your agenda. My 30/60/90-day plan was written before I was offered the job.*

Even before he officially stepped into his new role, Mike shared the plan with his new boss, who helped him fill in the blanks and schedule meetings with key executives whose support he would need to accomplish his goals. I asked Mike why he thinks the first 30 days of a CIO's tenure are so important. Here's what he told me:

Why are the first 30 days so important? They establish who you are, what you will do for the company, and how you will manage IT and the people in the IT organization.

Think about it: Immediately after you are announced as the new CIO, everyone goes to the Web to dig through your past, to see where you worked and to figure out who they might know who also knows you. That creates a situation where people—especially people in the IT organization—think they know something about you and start making guesses about what you'll do.

So in my first 30 days, I made sure to meet and spend time with each of my direct reports and with people one level down from there. In addition, I scheduled "town hall"–style meetings to make sure everyone got a chance to see me, to ask questions, and to understand my plans for IT.

During this time I was also meeting with every member of the senior leadership team and some of their direct reports. I also wrote an outline of questions for them and I used that outline as an introduction to help me understand what was on their minds, what was important to them from a business perspective and how I could help them. It's crucial to find a few things that can be addressed quickly to establish credibility.

Prior to joining Frontier, Mike had been at Unilever. As part of his management training there, he had spent three years with the company's international audit unit. It was a great experience that helped him see beyond the traditional horizons of IT.

At Unilever I learned that you always go in with a plan and with a set of questions that you send in advance. People have a limited amount of time, and it's much more effective to walk them through something they've already seen. It also says something about you when you come to a meeting fully prepared.

By front-loading the agendas of his early meetings, Mike was able to determine quickly what was important to his peers. It was a critical initial step toward building the trust he would need in the weeks, months, and years ahead.

You have to remember that most companies take many months, and sometimes years, to find the right person for the job. So you need to prove that you are the right person. Ideally, your first 30 days on the job establishes you as the leader and the personality who will guide the IT organization for years to come. It also indicates the level of success you are likely to achieve.

Mike reminded me that the CIO always has two key audiences, "your peers in the business and the people working for you in IT." Each audience requires a different management style, especially during the CIO's first weeks on the job.

First you try to understand what's important to the executive team in the near term and the long term. Then you figure out how IT can help them achieve those goals. Then you have to understand what's important to the business units across the enterprise, and figure out how IT can help them.

Basically, you're figuring out what the business needs, and then explaining it to IT, boiling it down to the ABCs and then filling in the blanks. These early steps are critical, because if you skip them, you're not setting yourself up for success.

" . . . always go in with a plan and with a set
of questions that you send in advance. People
have a limited amount of time, and it's much
more effective to walk them through something they've already seen. It also says something about you when you come to a meeting
fully prepared."

*And I've found that people really appreciate it when you are
prepared, when you have asked them questions, thought about
what you need to do, and come back to them with a plan for
action. This raises the comfort level. People are wondering
what you can do for them. People want to see that you've listened and that you've heard what they said. Remember, when
you meet with C-level executives, send the questions first and
then stick to the list. Don't make it a "meet and greet." That's
not why they hired you.*

Building trust is an essential part of the process of earning
the acceptance you will need to succeed over time. "People
get comfortable with you as you begin to demonstrate what
you can achieve," says Mike. "After you demonstrate your
value to people, their perception of you changes. They begin
inviting you to the important meetings and strategy discussions. You don't have to seek them out anymore—they begin
seeking you for your input and your advice."

I'm genuinely grateful to Mike for taking the time to walk
me through his preparation process. He was also kind
enough to share a scrubbed version of his 30-day plan. With
his permission, we're reproducing it here:

30-Day Plan

Before my official start date

- Contact key IT managers to establish rapport (if allowed)

- Set up time with admin to help prepare for my arrival

- Start setting up meetings with key stakeholders right away

- Set up first few meetings with key personnel until regular schedules are set

Week 1

Day 1—Headquarters

- HR—On-boarding requirements and paperwork

- Meet and greet people at HQ

- Call IT leads in other locations to introduce myself and confirm plans for visits in first few weeks

- Meet with my boss to go over his agenda and hot topics

- Get personal technology ready (laptop, printers, phone, mobile, etc.)

Day 2—Headquarters

- HQ—Get settled, office ready

- Meet with key stakeholders; understand their needs and strategies

- Review budget for IT

- Travel to other location

Day 3—Other location

- Breakfast with other location leads

- Meet with team leads—intros and key questions

- Introduction to the IT team at large—everyone!

- Lunch with team

- Overview sessions with other location lead, get to know environment

- Dinner with key personnel and/or team leads (any other key stakeholders)

Day 4—Other location

- IT leads present their areas of responsibility

  - Key customers internal/external

  - Projects, include business purpose, people, timelines, budget, and status

  - Key metrics for their areas of support

- Review organization structure and people; identify key team members

- Determine who is working on integration team and backfill requirements

- Continue to meet everyone

Day 5—Alternate corporate location

- Overview of integration project

- Schedule data center tour and review with outsourcer

- Travel home

- Report to boss

Week 2
Day 6—Headquarters

- Meet with boss—review assessments and thoughts

- Review urgent issues and business needs

- Continue to meet with key stakeholders

Day 7—Headquarters

- Continue to meet with key stakeholders

- Introduce myself to the top vendors and partners who support the organization—understand what they do, costs, metrics, performance, etc.

- Find out who manages the relationships with each of the vendor partners—how well is this managed?

- Travel to other location

Day 8—Other location

- Meet with other location lead on transition of responsibilities and developing his new role/agenda

- Continue understanding and involvement of the business transition plans

- Interview two to three of the longest-tenured people in the IT team—gain their insights on the history and views of what needs to be priority

- Interview two to three of the youngest people in the IT team—gain their insights of what works well and what needs to be enhanced for the next generation of workers

Day 9—Other location

- Continue to understand the organization structure and how things work (i.e., processes, SLAs, metrics, etc.)

- Review DR and business continuity planning

- Get an assessment of our customer service stats and continuous improvement efforts

- Continue to meet the team and other stakeholders

Day 10—Other location

- Review thoughts and ideas with all IT leaders.

- Communicate any observations, thoughts, and direction that need attention.

- Establish regular communication with leads and regular staff meeting agendas.

- Develop report for my boss on current status, assessments, and thoughts.

- Travel home.

Week 3

- Continue to understand the organization structure and how things work (i.e., processes, SLAs, metrics, etc.)

- Continue to meet with key stakeholders

- Introduce myself to the top vendors and partners who support us—understand what they do, costs, metrics, performance, etc.

- Understand the organization culture and how work gets from my boss up, down, and across the organization

- Focus on integration project with company acquisition—get involved, know who leads this, help

- Analyze and assess the IT organization—successes and failures—what needs attention?

  - Do we have the right structure/people/talent?

  - Are the processes working for the business?

  - Are the costs in line with the business requirements?

Week 4

- Continue as in Week 3—complete all early assessments:

  - IT organization—leadership and structure

  - Projects and planning

  - Ability to grow and take on the new company strategies

- From the understanding of the organization, start to put plans into action, create key messages, and communicate

Key Questions for the Interviews with Key Stakeholders
Strategy:

1. What is the strategy for the organization?

2. In what areas is the business most likely to face tough challenges in the next year or so?

3. What are the most promising opportunities for the business and for the industry for the next year or so?

People:

4. How do you measure success in the people who work for you and with you?

5. Let's say it's day one, and you and I are meeting; what will you tell me is the most imperative thing on your mind that I need to get busy on right away? What's the second?

6. Who are the key people or functions in the company that support your efforts?

Technology:

7. What is your view of IT in the past and the present? What makes IT successful or not?

8. What is your vision for IT in the future?

Culture:

9. Describe the culture of the organization.

10. What elements of the culture must be preserved?

11. What needs to change?

Move Quickly and Confidently

As a new CIO, you will be taking a hard look at your team. You will assess its strengths and weaknesses. You will figure out who on the team is going to help you—and who will hinder you. No matter how talented the team is that you inherit, you will probably be making some changes.

It's best to make these changes quickly—the longer you wait, the more difficult it becomes to act.

"As soon as you arrive on the job, people will be looking at you and wondering what you will do," says José Carlos Eiras, the former global CIO of General Motors Europe. "But your actions will depend on the quality of information available to you. Obviously, the people who interview you will give you their perspectives on IT, but that doesn't mean that their perspectives are accurate. Sometimes what you hear during the interview process doesn't reflect what's really going on. So you will have to find out the truth. You will need to discover the real situation very quickly, and then confront it."

Problems come in many varieties, and each situation is different. But when you find a problem that needs to be fixed, don't wait. "If you need to reduce costs or eliminate staff, it's better to do it right away," says José. "Do it carefully, but do it fast. Let the board know what you are doing so you keep their support. Paint an honest picture of the problems, and explain how your actions will improve the situation."

Once you have decided to act, resist the urge to delay. "The more time passes, the less confidence people will have in you," says José. Normally a new CIO is hired because there is something wrong with IT. So people expect you to move swiftly and decisively. The longer you wait, the harder it will be to create the level of confidence you need to make significant changes. The board will wonder when you're going to start delivering. The IT group will wonder when you're going

> " . . . people expect you to move swiftly and decisively. The longer you wait, the harder it will be to create the level of confidence you need to make significant changes. The board will wonder when you're going to start delivering. The IT group will wonder when you're going to start changing things. It's best to act quickly. Then you are free to move forward with your own strategy."

to start changing things. It's best to act quickly. Then you are free to move forward with your own strategy."

Harvey Koeppel, the former CIO of Citigroup's Global Consumer Group, agrees that it's crucial to convey a sense of confidence and strength in the first weeks on the job. "You need to declare yourself very early on . . . so people understand clearly who you are and what you stand for . . . you must establish yourself as a credible business leader."

If you fail to send the right messages during those initial weeks, you risk damaging your credibility as a leader. "You don't want to be perceived as a tactical manager, somebody who only cares about keeping the e-mail running. It's critical for you to be seen as a business leader—someone who delivers results that grow the business," says Harvey.

For a new CIO, delivering results means focusing on short-term, achievable victories. "It's not about some grandiose two-year or three-year programs," says Harvey. "It's about continuous net improvement, a series of small things that you can accomplish this week or next month. It's about showing your customers and your colleagues that you know how to leverage technology to improve their lives."

Helping your customers and colleagues *right now* is what's important, says Harvey. "The age of the five-year project is dead. The world changes too quickly."

Focusing on short-term wins will actually improve your chances of achieving long-term success, because it's the small victories that people tend to remember. Those are the victories that build support for you, within the IT organization and across the enterprise.

Alter Perceptions

Those first 30 days are also a perfect time to begin changing perceptions about IT, both inside and outside the IT organization. John Phillips is currently the CIO at Briggs Medical Service Company. He shared a great story from earlier in his career at a different firm, when he turned a chronic IT skeptic into a trusted partner by listening carefully, and then acting promptly.

> *I was the CIO at a large, publicly traded company . . . and in my first 30 days there I met with the heads of all the business units. There was one particular executive who told me he didn't particularly like IT, no matter who was running it. And I said to him, "What would change your mind to get you to like IT?" He said, "If I could just get a PC on an employee's desk within three days after we ask for it . . . "*

As you can imagine, we kept a very close watch on the help desk and when the first ticket for a PC came in from an employee from that division, we got the PC on that employee's desk the next day. Well, that made an immediate difference in our relationship with the executive. And that, in turn, enabled us to move forward and form a closer and more effective partnership with that business unit because now they had a different perception of IT.

From John's perspective, the first 30 days offers a window of opportunity for winning hearts and minds across the enterprise—and within the IT organization itself. He has a seven-point IT Value System that he uses to shift perceptions internally:

1. Focus on the customer first.

2. Overcommunicate wherever and whenever possible.

3. Take ownership—passing the responsibility does not relieve the accountability.

4. Build committed teams that work together.

5. Champion the cause—become proactive leaders.

6. Defend the champions —"get behind it."

7. Enjoy your career—if you're not excited about coming to work, then don't.

I think that John makes a critical point: Changing attitudes and perceptions within IT is the first step in transforming the broader relationship between the IT organization and the rest of the enterprise. And I agree that it makes sense to get started soon—in those first 30 days.

> ## Lesson
>
> Focusing on short-term wins will actually improve your chances of achieving long-term success, because it's the small victories that people tend to remember. Those are the victories that build support for you, within the IT organization and across the enterprise.

"If you don't, then it's like running in mud," says John. "You'll be working real hard, but you're not going to get a lot of traction or make a lot of progress."

Tone Matters

Yuri Aguiar is a senior partner and CIO at Ogilvy & Mather Worldwide. Finding the right leadership tone in the first 30 days, he says, is not an option—it's an imperative. "If you are hired as a CIO, you are hired to lead; hence not establishing a leadership tone is *not* an option. Building relationships with the business leaders and forging genuine partnerships is *mandatory*. Building trust will take much longer, and will depend in a large way on execution, delivery and transparency within the partnerships that are forged early on."

Here is a great story from Yuri illustrating the need to set the right tone from the get-go:

I vividly recollect one situation that started Day 14 on the job and took a few months to play out.

I had a one-on-one meeting with a senior executive. In the midst of my articulating what I thought would be a good way forward, he candidly reminded me that he'd heard it all before and he really needed to see results from the team. I considered this a formidable challenge as he was extremely technology-savvy and could read through any false pretexts.

With the help of a couple of sharp members of the technology team, we identified two serious challenges within his business unit and set out to address them. We kept the effort relatively low key as the team worked through them. Four months later, when all was said and done, we had people from within the business unit present the resolutions at a review meeting.

The conversation after that was very different. We managed to build trust where little existed before and now the executive is a close advisor to the technology team . . . and he keeps us abreast of his business plans on a regular basis.

Yuri also helped to see a vital connection between the ability to interpret group dynamics quickly and the ability to lead successfully. Here are his remarks:

Since people are the foundation of any great technology department, understanding the structure and dynamics of the group is key. How the group understands the business imperatives of the organization and how they interpret them within a technology strategy must be understood in the early days of engagement.

Mildly misinterpreting working dynamics of a group or the company's business objectives can have far-reaching implications. Everything from restructuring efforts to technology strategy and related tactics can have devastating results in the medium term. A few degrees off course at the beginning may not seem like much, but 500 miles down the road it would lead to a very different destination.

Technology Last

We interviewed many CIOs to gather their impressions about the first 30 days on the job. When we read through the interview transcripts, we were struck by their complete agreement on one point: The technology itself is the last thing you have to worry about.

What emerged from the interviews was a clear sense that a new CIO must focus on building trust, building confidence, and building relationships—inside and outside of the IT organization—during the first critical weeks on the job.

"The first thirty days set the tone," says Mark H. Griesbaum, a longtime CIO who recently became president of TCS Online Services. "They give the IT organization a sense of what is important to you as a leader. They provide the business with a sense of whether you grasp the company's key priorities and understand how IT can best meet those needs."

Don't expect people to beat a path to your door just to shake your hand. As a new CIO, your top priority should be reaching out.

"Communicate, communicate, communicate," says Mark. "Build relationships with your customers across the organization. Listen carefully to what people are telling you. Focus on what is critical to them, and remember why you were hired in

> "Focusing on technology is the biggest mis-
> take a CIO can make. People don't care about
> the details of technology, they care about
> whether you understand the business and
> you can add value to strategically improve
> your company and the services it provides to
> its customers."

the first place—you must have had a set of competencies that set you apart from your predecessor and from the other candidates who applied for the job."

For a new CIO, says Mark, a key task is learning what the business needs. "Focusing on technology is the biggest mistake a CIO can make. People don't care about the details of technology, they care about whether you understand the business and you can add value to strategically improve your company and the services it provides to its customers."

Each company is different, and each will have its own unique sets of issues and priorities. Your job as CIO is figuring out which priorities must be addressed today, and which can wait until tomorrow. Then you need to figure out the best way of explaining to everyone how you determined which projects will be pursued now and which projects will be pursued later.

Don't be mysterious—be transparent and forthcoming. Explain your reasons, and invite people to engage in a

> ## Lesson
>
> A new CIO must focus on building trust, building confidence, and building relationships—inside and outside of the IT organization—during the first critical weeks on the job.

dialogue with you. Even when they disagree with you, they are more likely to respect you if they believe that you have honestly listened to their side of the story.

Building from Scratch

The first time I heard Greg Fell describe his first 30 days on the job as "unique," I thought that he might be exaggerating. He was not. Greg has a terrific story to tell about his early days as CIO at Terex Corp.

"Here was a Fortune 500 company that didn't have a CIO or an IT organization," says Fell. "We had to build an IT organization from scratch, and launch an ambitious global ERP project to support management's goal of transforming Terex from a holding company into an operating company."

Terex Corporation is a leading global manufacturer of heavy equipment used in many industries, including construction, infrastructure, quarrying, mining, shipping, transportation, energy, and refining. In 2005, Terex embarked on a large-scale effort to unify the company's multiple operating units under a single brand. The transformation process would make it easier for Terex customers to do business with the company. It would also enable Terex to leverage its size and scale to become more efficient and more competitive.

But transformation would be complex, and IT would play a key role in ensuring its success. Here's the story, in Greg's own words:

> *When I was hired, the corporate office had fewer than 70 people. Most of them were lawyers and accountants. There were only two people in corporate IT. The rest of the IT people were scattered across 50 manufacturing sites. We had no networks connecting the sites, not even a common e-mail system. One of the division presidents was using an AOL.com address for his business e-mail. Everything was run locally, so it was difficult to track down reliable information or get questions answered. We didn't have what most companies would consider an IT infrastructure.*
>
> *So we had to build everything from scratch: common business processes, an ERP system, a program management office, a global network to share information. I think this really was a unique situation for a Fortune 500 CIO. I had a clean slate, a blank sheet of paper.*
>
> *In addition to building IT systems, we also had to create a supply chain process, a marketing process, and a lean manufacturing process.*
>
> *On the upside, we had very few legacy issues. So we could focus on the critical systems that were absolutely necessary and we could be highly efficient. On the downside, however, I had no predecessor to blame when something went wrong.*

Over the next four years, the company doubled in size, and the IT organization grew significantly. "When I worked at Ford Motor Co., we had an IT organization with about 10,000 people. Here at Terex, we've got about 400 people in IT, but I'm happy to say that we're extremely efficient. It's truly a unique situation."

Greg credits his previous experience at Ford and his business savvy as key factors in his success at Terex. "Your knowledge of technology is the price of admission, but your success depends on your ability to understand the business and help it grow."

Chapter 7

CIO Evolution

Executive Summary

As much as I relish the idea of presenting you with some sort of George Jetson-esque image depicting the *CIO of TO-MORROW*, complete with a flying car, the plain truth is that the future state of the CIO is already visible. As you would suspect, it's less about technology than it is about mind-set. What makes the CIO of the future different from the CIO of the present isn't storage capacity or run rates—it's the willingness to work outside the comfort zone of IT and embrace the challenges of business.

Keeping It Simple

Just a few days before we sent the manuscript for *The Transformational CIO* to our editor at Wiley, we had the opportunity to interview Patrick Toole, the CIO of IBM. Although I was tempted to save Pat's interview for my *next* book, his input and insight were so valuable that I felt they had to be included in this book. I hope you'll agree that I made the right choice.

I caught up with Pat at the IBM offices in North Castle, a picturesque town of 12,000 in a section of Westchester County that still resembles a primeval forest. Pat has worked at IBM since 1984. Several years ago, his father retired from IBM. In many respects, Pat seems like the epitome of a traditional "IBMer." But appearances can be deceiving. In reality, Pat represents the future of IBM—and in many respects, he also represents the future of IT leadership.

"It's all about the business," says Pat. "At the end of the day, we're driven by outcomes. For IT, what matters most are business results. And not just this quarter's business results, but the next quarter and the next year and the next five years. That's what drives us. It's in our DNA."

> "It's all about the business. At the end of the day, we're driven by outcomes. For IT, what matters most are business results. And not just this quarter's business results, but the next quarter and the next year and the next five years. That's what drives us. It's in our DNA."

Pat also represents a new evolutionary stage in the IBM organizational structure. Until as recently as January 2009, IBM had multiple CIOs. "Historically, every business unit had its own CIO," Pat explains. "At one point, we had 128 CIOs in the company!"

But Sam Palmisano had other ideas. As IBM's chairman, CEO, and president, Sam knew that IBM had to become a truly unified enterprise to remain a leader in the worldwide economy. Early in his tenure as CEO, Sam launched a multi-year, enterprise-wide strategy to transform the company into an integrated, collaborative, and highly efficient global organization. The team guiding that ambitious strategy is led by Pat and his boss, Linda Sanford. Linda is IBM's senior vice president of enterprise transformation, a title that accurately describes her role as an architect of substantive change.

So far, the transformation team has helped IBM post record earnings, despite the rocky economy. The team recently committed to what IBM describes as "an aggressive plan to drive more growth over the next five years" and "shave an additional $8 billion" off the company's $78 billion in total expenses by 2015. That's a tall order, but with everyone in IT pulling in the same direction, it's achievable.

The team's list of transformation projects includes a streamlined approach for setting up IT infrastructure at new IBM sites that dramatically reduces the time required to get new locations up and running; globally integrated support functions for HR, finance, legal, and other service areas that eliminate redundancies and diminished spending by $4 billion in the past four years; and a massive IT assessment, resulting in the elimination of more than 10,000 nonstrategic internal software applications and the consolidation of thousands of servers onto mainframes and 155 data centers down to a mere five.

Keeping IT tightly aligned with the company's business goals is an essential part of IBM's overall strategy. Pat describes his formula for maintaining that close alignment between IT and the business in one word: simplicity.

At IBM, the IT organization focuses on achieving measurable business outcomes in three broad areas:

1. Earnings per share (EPS)

2. Enterprise risk management (ERM)

3. Strategic projects

Pat estimates that about half of the IT organization's resources are focused on helping the company meet its EPS objectives, which are spelled out clearly in a public

> ## Lesson
>
> Pat estimates that about half of the IT organization's re-sources are focused on helping the company meet its EPS objectives, which are spelled out clearly in a public document. "Our focus on EPS establishes a very direct connection between IT and shareholder value."

document. "Our focus on EPS establishes a very direct con-nection between IT and shareholder value," says Pat.

Tight Linkage Ensures Buy-In

The tight linkage between IT activities and real-world busi-ness objectives also ensures high levels of buy-in and support from the company's senior leadership. For example, several current projects are aligned with sales force productivity, which is always a top concern at large global companies op-erating in highly competitive markets.

"We have one new tool that identifies 'white space accounts' (i.e., potential new customers), and provides con-tact information and even selling scripts," says Pat. "It's a great example of leveraging technology to improve sales productiv-ity. We took an ad hoc process and made it measurable, so now we know exactly which deals and opportunities resulted from using the tool. We can actually see the sales pipeline growing, thanks to the tool's analytics."

Another IT initiative involved creating a new tool to speed the hand-off of qualified leads from marketers to business

Lesson

The tight linkage between IT activities and real-world business objectives also ensures high levels of buy-in and support from the company's senior leadership. Several current projects are aligned with sales force productivity, which is always a top concern at large global companies operating in highly competitive markets.

partners. "By automating it, we were able to shave five days off the process," says Pat. "That savings in time actually helped us increase our share in some markets, because the leads weren't getting stale. We will do anything we can do to make the sales process more efficient."

Pat keeps a close eye on the status of IT initiatives with a dashboard that displays progress, costs, promised benefits, and other key metrics. "I review the status of our initiatives with our team on a monthly basis, but it's great that I can use the dashboard to check the progress of an initiative at any time."

IT also invests significantly in the development of large strategic projects "that will move the needle over the next 10 to 20 years," says Pat. "That's our investment in the future."

ERM currently represents a smaller portion of total IT investment, but the importance of ERM-related activities is likely to grow as regulatory environments worldwide become stricter. "The whole area of compliance, especially for global

> ## Lesson
>
> Pat keeps a close eye on the status of IT initiatives with a dashboard that displays progress, costs, promised benefits, and other key metrics.

companies, has become incredibly complex. You can't keep on top of it unless you automate a lot of the processes," says Pat.

When you're talking with Pat, you get the feeling that you're not talking to the typical CIO—he sounds more like the VP of a business unit!

Pat obviously gets it—he understands that the role of the CIO and the role of IT have changed permanently. When I ask him how he manages to convey that sense of awareness to the rest of the IT organization, he reemphasizes the importance of simplicity.

Pat's organizational style is uncomplicated and direct. IT is organized into three basic teams:

1. Run

2. Transform

3. Integrate

"The Run team does just that—it runs the operations of IT. The Transform team makes sure the initiatives line up with the business. The Integrate team makes sure that everything works together across the enterprise process centers, the business units and the geographies," Pat explains.

Augmenting those three fundamental teams are an enterprise architecture team, an operations team, and an innovation team (see the following graphic). For a large group within one of the largest companies in the world, that's a remarkably simple table of organization!

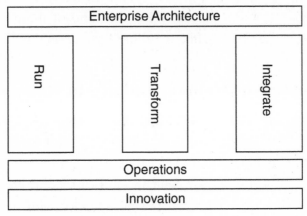

Table of Organization

When I ask Pat what worries him, he just smiles. Then he describes what would probably seem like Nirvana to most IT professionals:

There are plenty of things that keep me energized and excited. We have a center of excellence that we call "Workplace of the Future." We're looking at all the aspects of being an IBMer and how we work. We're thinking about how we provision our people so they can be as productive and as effective as possible. From an IT perspective, that opens up so many exciting possibilities, everything from processes to devices. We're thinking about all the ways to improve collaboration so people can work together seamlessly, no matter where they are. It's a tremendous opportunity, very exciting. That's what motivates me.

My conversation with Pat reinforced my idea that there are two basic "camps" of CIOs. In one camp are the CIOs who see themselves primarily as custodians of IT. In the other camp are the CIOs who see themselves as business leaders. I cannot help but think that one of these camps represents the past, while the other represents the future.

Transitioning from Operational to Strategic

Shortly after speaking with Pat, I had a great conversation with Diana Melick. Diana is the former CIO of Siemens Energy and Automation, a $4 billion business unit within Siemens AG, the global giant in electronics and electrical engineering. Now she is a business leader with full P&L responsibility at Siemens IT Solutions & Services. Her combination of technology and business experience gives her a unique perspective on the future state of the CIO.

I asked her if CIOs had developed a rule of thumb to determine the right amounts of time to spend on operations and strategy. Here's what she told me:

You have to be operational. That's an important part of the job. No matter how you look at it, you will probably spend a quarter of your time making sure that your projects are moving ahead, that your environments are up and running, that the business is getting what it needs. Operations is a critical element, and there's no getting around it.

But then you have to carve out a larger portion of your time to spend with the business. You need to work on strategy and planning. They're also critical. You can't ignore them.

I don't have a great answer in terms of an exact percentage, but you can't be spending a large amount of your time on operations. It's got to be 25 percent, or less. If you're spending 40 percent of your time on operations, you're not going to be around very long.

There used to be a lot of CIOs who spent most of their career just trying to keep things quiet and managing operations. Today's world is different—much more is required and requested of the CIO. You just can't focus all of your time and energy on operations.

An excellent way to transition from a largely operational role into a more strategic role is by volunteering to lead or co-chair company-wide initiatives. Diana shared a great example with me:

When I was CIO, we had a set of five or six strategic company initiatives proposed by the executive team. They asked for volunteers who would lead the programs. I volunteered to lead the customer focus program. For my co-leader, I picked a very respected figure in the company, the VP of communications. I figured it was a good partnership for what we were trying to accomplish, which was making it easier for customers to do business with Siemens.

We scoped out the whole program. We outlined it and asked ourselves, "What do we really need to do to make this work?" We ran it past the CEO and the CFO, because they determined which projects would go forward. We got their agreement that our program truly was one of the key strategic initiatives that should go forward.

Then we held external focus groups with our customers. We got the feedback from our key distributors, identifying exactly what things we needed to improve on. We ran prototype sessions past them, of the work that we had done before we released it, so we made them a part of the process of making it easier to do business with us. I think that was really, really beneficial. We also had to understand what our competitors were doing in this area and understand the marketplace and the solutions.

And then we drove the customer focus program for the company. One of the reasons it was very successful was the joint partnership between IT, the business, and our customers. It was done purely on a strategic level. It was fun to work on. It's the kind of project that CIOs should be involved in, because it can make a huge *impact on the bottom line.*

I love this story because it illustrates how a forward-looking CIO can transform the company, transform IT, and transform herself—all at the same time!

I think people viewed me more as a strategy partner instead of an operational CIO whom they called when they had issues. When I worked on the customer focus project, we engaged in a different type of discussion. We were talking about how to improve the customer experience, how to improve collaboration with the customer, how to improve

"I volunteered to lead the customer focus program. For my co-leader, I picked a very respected figure in the company, the VP of communications. . . . It was a good partnership . . . "

transactions with end customers, how to sell better, and how to sell more to the customers. So it allowed me to engage with the business on a completely different level of discussion. We weren't talking about the ERP system, we were talking about growing the company.

From Diana's perspective, the transformational CIO is a C-level executive who knows how to use technology to drive business, reduce costs, streamline operations, and make it easier for the company's customers to do business with the company.

Diana is too modest to say this, but I believe that her track record of successful strategic business partnerships was one of the reasons that she was elevated to a leadership role at one of the company's most important business units.

In the end, that's really what it's all about—having the intelligence, the desire, and the courage to change. The CIO community has been talking for years about having a seat at the table. From my perspective, the very image of a bunch of chairs and a table seems old fashioned.

> "When I worked on the customer focus proj-
> ect, we engaged in a different type of discus-
> sion. We were talking about how to improve
> the customer experience . . . it allowed me
> to engage with the business on a completely
> different level of discussion. We weren't
> talking about the ERP system, we were talk-
> ing about growing the company."

What matters now, more than ever, is the CIO's vision, the CIO's willingness to lead change, and the CIO's ability to work with the business as a trusted partner.

The CIO doesn't need a "seat" in a boardroom because the CIO can add value to the organization from anywhere in the world, at any time. That's the proper role of the trans-formational CIO—understanding the present, anticipating the future, and enabling the business to compete successfully no matter how much the world around it changes.

And if there's one thing you can bet on, it's that the world will keep changing. But look on the bright side—that means no shortage of work for the transformational CIO.

Chapter 8

The Road Ahead

Executive Summary

The "do more with less" conversation has run its course. Cost optimization and efficiency will always remain priorities, but they are no longer the company's *top* priorities. More and more, the conversation between corporate management and the CIO is focused on business growth. Everyone looks to the CIO and asks: How will you help us grow the business? For the CIO, the road ahead points to a fuller and more dynamic relationship with the business. IT will be expected to provide new services and new capabilities that will enable the company's growth strategies.

So the next logical question is: *Which* technologies and *which* strategies will provide the foundational support for the various new services and new capabilities that the business will undoubtedly demand?

A Time for IT Leadership

Every year, I speak with literally *thousands* of senior-level corporate executives. It's part of my role at HMG Strategy. Some of the conversations are deep and some are perfunctory. The quality of a conversation can be influenced by many variables, including the background of the person I'm chatting with, the topic we're discussing, the time of day, and even the time of year. You can never predict exactly where a conversation will go.

Around the middle part of last year, however, I noticed a trend. Many of the conversations were falling into one of three buckets: cloud, mobile, or social computing. I sensed a harbinger of dramatic change. I wrote an article about it for my newsletter. The headline was *New "Perfect Storm" Will Transform IT Industry and Global Economy*. Here's the article:

A new "perfect storm" is on the horizon. The convergence of cloud, mobile, and social computing is reshaping the world we live in, and transforming the IT industry as we know it.

Make no mistake: This new convergence is driving the most significant transformation of IT since we put PCs on everyone's desk. This phenomenon is so big that we cannot even begin to guess at the magnitude of the change that will occur. The ripples and aftershocks will be just as transformational as the first wave of changes that we are experiencing now.

In many ways, this new convergence will be even more transformative than the arrival of desktop computing more than two decades ago. Like the desktop revolution, which ended the dominance of the mainframe centralized computing, the convergence of cloud, mobile and social computing will permanently alter the landscape.

There will be a host of unforeseen consequences, unexpected challenges and marvelous opportunities for nimble organizations with the courage to endure the storm.

In the same way that desktop computing made it possible for everyone with a spreadsheet program to create their own versions of the "truth," the convergence of cloud, mobile and social computing will undoubtedly create its own batch of interesting problems.

But the new convergence is also likely to re-energize large patches of the global economy by opening new markets and creating lucrative new business opportunities all over the world.

For those of us in IT leadership, this represents the chance of a lifetime. If we step up, if we speak up, if we assume responsibility, we can determine the shape and form of the future. New architectures, new processes and new skills will be required to support the new convergence. It's our job as IT leaders to set the tone and articulate the vision for the transformed IT industry that will invariably emerge from the convergence of cloud, mobile and social computing.

In retrospect, I should have included strategic global sourcing among the converging trends, because it's impossible to escape the feeling that Tom Friedman had it right when he wrote *The World Is Flat.*

Today, the sensation that we are standing at the precipice of a new era seems even stronger than it did when I wrote the article six months ago. The magnitude and potential impact of these converging trends is truly amazing.

Playing down the importance of these trends is like trying to play down the force of a hurricane. Ignoring the storm won't make it go away or reduce its awesome power. I live a stone's throw from the Long Island Sound, and when a nor'-easter heads our way, we don't pretend that it's not coming—we get ready and we make sure that we're prepared.

Figuring Out What's Relevant

Sheila Jordan is vice president of communications and collaboration IT at Cisco. In her role at Cisco, she has a broad portfolio of responsibilities. One of them is making sure that IT initiatives are aligned and integrated with business strategy across the company. She is also part of the team that developed and launched Cisco Quad, the company's new enterprise collaboration platform. The platform combines social networking with communications, business information, and content management systems.

So perhaps it's natural that when you ask Sheila to name a technology that will play a significant role in shaping the future of IT, she's likely to say, "Enterprise collaboration." I think it's probably best if she explains why in her own words:

Today the business is saying that it needs to get to market faster, that it needs a rapid mechanism for keeping pace with all the changes in our global economy. And at the same time, the business needs constant input to make sure that it produces and delivers goods and services that the market really wants.

Global high-performance teams are critical components of the "rapid mechanism" that Sheila describes. In the same way that the platoon is the fundamental unit of the Marine Corps, the global high-performance team is the fundamental unit of the modern global corporation.

In addition to being cross-functional and cross-cultural, the global high-performance team—as its name implies—is made up of individuals who live and work in different parts of the world. Global teams enable the business to deliver against all the new requirements of a global marketplace.

But global teams can't work without robust, user-friendly technologies for sharing and disseminating information, quickly and securely. That's where enterprise collaboration comes into the picture—it's the glue that keeps the global enterprise from flying apart.

Enterprise collaboration platforms often include tools that are similar to popular features on social networking sites such as Facebook and Twitter. Because they are already familiar to many people, these kinds of social tools can be learned and adopted quickly when they are repurposed for business functions.

Lesson

Global teams can't work without robust, user-friendly technologies for sharing and disseminating information, quickly and securely.

So while the user interface of an enterprise collaboration platform might *look* like a social media web site, the resemblance is only skin-deep. In any event, the goal of enterprise collaboration isn't recreating Facebook or Twitter—the goal is enabling the global high-performance teams that are essential to succeed in a global economy. As Sheila says:

This isn't about collaboration just for the sake of collaborating. It's about understanding the behaviors of people who are already using social technologies to communicate and to share information—and bringing all of that into the enterprise. Enterprise collaboration is where social collaboration meets work; it's where we use social technologies to optimize critical business processes.

From an IT perspective, we need to embrace what's happening—embrace, but filter at the same time. The consumerization of IT is happening and it would be silly to ignore it.

We have to figure out what's important and what's appropriate in the business world. Again, it's not just about collaborating—it's about determining which behaviors and which tools have real business relevancy inside the enterprise.

The end users might be saying they want Facebook and they want Twitter, but that's not necessarily exactly what they want. What they really want are the capabilities. They

"This isn't about collaboration just for the sake of collaborating. It's about understanding the behaviors of people who are already using social technologies to communicate and to share information—and bringing all of that into the enterprise."

want the user-friendly features and functionalities of social media, but they want them integrated and tied into their business systems.

Sheila speaks passionately and knowledgeably about enterprise collaboration and all the various technologies supporting it. I'm glad that she agreed to be interviewed for this book, because her message is important. For example, she also sees the "mind-set of IT" changing as newer technologies, such as enterprise collaboration and cloud computing, play larger roles in enabling key business processes:

We all know there's this massive trend happening in the IT industry. We're moving to services—delivering services to the organization. To me, that is a phenomenal and transformational trend within the IT industry.

But it also means you have to change the mind-set of the IT organization. IT has to start thinking like an organization that provides services to its client base.

In the past, IT delivered projects or applications or technologies. We didn't step back and ask ourselves, "What are we really delivering for our client base?"

We didn't view IT as part of an overall experience. I specifically use the word "experience" because thinking in terms of the overall experience is what will help us change the mindset of IT.

When IT delivers something, I want to make sure that we're delivering a collective experience for our end users, an experience that helps them become more productive.

The challenge for CIOs is changing how IT is perceived in the enterprise, and changing how IT perceives itself. Everyone expects IT to deliver services faster, better, and cheaper. Now we also have to start delivering services that will help the business grow.

Sheila envisions three "wins" that enterprise collaboration systems can deliver value to the business:

1. Productivity/Efficiency

2. Innovation

3. Growth

It's relatively easy to convince senior management that enterprise collaboration solutions can improve productivity

> "The challenge for CIOs is changing how IT is perceived in the enterprise, and changing how IT perceives itself. Everyone expects IT to deliver services faster, better, and cheaper. Now we also have to start delivering services that will help the business grow."

and efficiency, since most people can immediately see the potential for saving time and money by using videoconferencing and other newer technologies that enable communication among remote workers.

It might be more difficult convincing senior management that enterprise collaboration can help the business drive innovation and growth. So it will be up to the CIO, with the help of the vendor community, to develop case studies showing the business benefits of enterprise collaboration.

That being said, it's safe to assume that enterprise collaboration will be a driving force in the next round of business transformation. The proliferation of collaborative tools—with or without the approval of top management—will surely cause headaches for the CIO. To minimize the pain, CIOs should start thinking now about how to integrate collaboration technologies with existing enterprise architectures.

Lesson

It's safe to assume that enterprise collaboration will be a driving force in the next round of business transformation. CIOs should start thinking now about how to integrate collaboration technologies with existing enterprise architectures.

It certainly would be foolish to relive the "bad old days" of early CRM implementations, in which new technologies were brought in through the side door without IT's knowledge or blessing. I think it's safe to say that no CIO wants to experience that kind of scenario.

Taking a nonintegrated or "hands-off" approach to collaboration is unlikely to prove beneficial in the long run. If each department winds up buying its own collaboration tools, new silos are likely to emerge around those tools. "That would defeat the purpose of collaboration," says Sheila. "It might make it easier for teams within a department to collaborate, but in the end, you wouldn't have an enterprise system enabling real global collaboration among all of the company's employees, customers, stakeholders and partners."

Hot and Getting Hotter

Lee Congdon is the CIO at Red Hat, a global leader in open source software and services. He sees the move to cloud-based services as a true "paradigm shift," right up there with the transition from mainframes to minis, the introduction of the PC, and the emergence of e-commerce.

I'm inclined to agree with him. The cloud is hot, and getting hotter. If we haven't reached a tipping point yet, we will soon. When you ask Lee how much of the IT infrastructure can be safely moved into the cloud today, his initial response is: "everything." He adds quickly that it all depends on the organization, but his confidence and enthusiasm are undeniable. Here's the way Lee sees it, in his own words:

Most enterprises already outsource some things to the cloud. Procurement, payroll, benefits, banking, travel, Web conferencing, etc. I think it's a rare enterprise today that doesn't have something that could be called a cloud application of some sort.

That said, outsourcing to the cloud will be difficult for a lot of enterprises, particularly those that are highly regulated or not rewarded for taking risks, and those that have limited financial resources. Many enterprises haven't built up the skills or the capabilities for moving operations into the cloud. Your application interfaces and your architecture may need to be recrafted, and that takes work.

Cloud application management is still evolving. There are point solutions and tools that provide a good set of capabilities for various environments, but there's still lots of work to be done.

Lee's advice is straightforward: Begin preparing now for the inevitable shift toward cloud computing.

Start developing knowledge, kicking the tires, understanding vendor strategy, and understanding who the players are. Start thinking about what your business needs are and identifying business partners that may be willing to invest or take additional risk to derive business value from the cloud.

Look at your application portfolio and pick something that's a likely candidate to move into the cloud. Pick something that's aging or brand new, or something where there's some flexibility on the delivery. And don't forget to address the risks. You will need to find additional business value to justify being a pioneer with some of these applications.

I think you have to use a portfolio management technique and pick your applications carefully. Test the waters. Remember that your regulators and auditors have probably built their processes and procedures around existing infrastructure, so there will typically be a lag before they're comfortable with auditing and providing guidance in a new environment. All these are things to think about.

I think Lee has it right. Test the waters. Proceed with caution. But definitely move forward. I really don't think there's a choice—if you don't take advantage of the cloud, your competitors surely will.

"You need the capability and capacity to change," says Lee. "I think an IT organization needs to be investing right now and ensuring they've got the capabilities to start moving to the cloud. In my view, a lot of these cloud applications will add value for most enterprises. Of course, it will take time to migrate existing workloads to the cloud. As I mentioned, this is a paradigm shift. If you aren't preparing already, you need to be moving in this direction."

"Start developing knowledge, kicking the tires, understanding vendor strategy, and understanding who the players are. Start thinking about what your business needs are and identifying business partners that may be willing to invest or take additional risk to derive business value from the cloud."

Challenges and Caveats

The short-term advantages of cloud-based apps are fairly obvious: Low initial cost and lots of prebuilt functionality. That means you can use the cloud as an innovation platform, a virtual test bed for experimenting with new techniques and new processes.

"It can be a very inexpensive platform," says Lee. "You only need a few pennies to lease a Linux machine in the cloud. You can also take advantage of software as a service (SaaS) apps from companies like Salesforce.com and Google."

There are downside risks, however. Interoperability is likely to crop up as an issue, at least in the initial stages. Security will be a challenge. When your data is spread across the cloud, how do you make certain that it's safe and secure? How do you move big chunks of it back and forth when you need it?

Vendor lock-in will be another issue to confront. What happens when vendors develop their own unique proprietary cloud solutions? Will these proprietary systems limit choice and reduce flexibility? Naturally enough, Lee encourages IT decision makers to consider open-source solutions as a way to avoid vendor lock-in. Clearly, there's a lot to think about.

There's little doubt, however, that the rapid consumerization of technology will drive more and more companies into the cloud, because that's where they'll find the inexpensive apps they need to satisfy the ever-changing demands of their end users.

> ### Lesson
>
> Interoperability is likely to crop up as an issue, at least in the initial stages. Security will be a challenge. When your data is spread across the cloud, how do you make certain that it's safe and secure? How do you move big chunks of it back and forth when you need it?

Don't discount the force of social pressure on IT strategy. Remember that the next wave of employees and customers will emerge from a generation of kids who learned how to use laptops, notebooks, and smart phones before they entered preschool.

The End of "Inside" versus "Outside"

Andy Lark is vice president of marketing for the Large Enterprise Group at Dell. His role gives him a spectacular vantage point from which to view the global transformation of IT. According to Andy, most CIOs are ready to embrace change—but they just aren't sure how to do it.

"I've found that for the most part, CIOs and CTOs are flexible, enthusiastic, and willing to embrace change. They are *very* ready to embrace change," says Andy. "But the challenge for them is embracing change while at the same time protecting the context of the business. This is a very complex scenario and there's a lot of risk involved."

Andy says he detects a distinct level of naïveté around cloud computing, due in no small part to the hype surrounding it. Here's his take on the current situation, in his own words:

I just came back from an event in Australia, where you've got every major cloud vendor down there touting cloud at a buck a gigabyte, or whatever it might be. That's a very attractive value proposition.

I spoke to some of the CIOs at the event and I asked them, "Where's the data going to be stored?" "Singapore," they said. I asked if that would meet their security policies. "No, the data is not allowed to leave the country," they told me. From my perspective, that seems like a bit of a problem.

Then I asked, "What's the security protocol for moving the data around?" and they said, "Well, there isn't one." And I said, "So you're okay with that?" and they said, "No, we can't do that." Seems like another problem, right?

Suddenly, the cloud doesn't look like such a great bargain. As it turns out, the services are priced at pretty much what they're worth.

That's why CIOs are having a hard time getting their heads around this. CIOs deal with the real world, not the world of fiction. The real cloud is a different world altogether, with real infrastructure, real investments, real everything. It's not just about chic.

I asked Andy whether there is a reasonable middle path that enables the CIO to move forward and embrace the future without putting critical systems at risk. Here's his reply:

Companies moving into the cloud are doing it on a workload basis. They're not moving their entire enterprise to the cloud, they're moving very specific applications and very specific workloads to the cloud. They're doing it in a very considered way, a very mature and managed way.

Many of these companies are looking at hybrid environments. They're looking at moving secondary data storage backup to the cloud. Or they're moving e-mail archival to the cloud. They're taking incremental steps, getting their toes wet first by moving components, rather than entire systems, to the cloud.

And by the way, moving those components and workloads to the cloud can represent significant savings. You can reduce a good chunk of your costs. A great example of this is large-scale, Web-based application testing. In some companies, as much as 20 percent of the IT infrastructure is dedicated to application testing and development. Now let's say you can go and test your applications in the cloud. It might sound like just dipping a toe in the water, but it eliminates a major chunk of your infrastructure and application costs.

So I would say there are CIOs who are embracing the cloud on the basis of what may look like very small investments on the surface but represent, in reality, very large and very significant parts of their workload.

> "Companies moving into the cloud are doing it on a workload basis. They're not moving their entire enterprise to the cloud, they're moving very specific applications and very specific workloads to the cloud. They're doing it in a very considered way, a very mature and managed way."

After chatting with Sheila, Lee, and Andy, I'm convinced that cloud, mobile, and social computing are driven by the same gale-force winds. I really like how Andy describes the shifting landscape:

> *The enterprise has become a highly social environment with very few barriers between the "inside" and the "outside." There has been a huge democratization of technology. Anybody can have the equivalent of a notebook computer sitting in the palm of their hand. One swipe of a credit card can bring you virtually infinite storage capacity. These are absolutely real challenges facing IT.*
>
> *The notion that the IT department can "control" the IT experience has gone out the door. If you say to a user right now, "You can't use Facebook in here, it's not an approved application," they'll simply bring their own computer to work and find a wifi network they can access.*

Andy's words ring true. The "perfect storm" isn't just taking place at the enterprise level—it's having an impact everywhere!

> *It goes right down to the level of the device. Someone you hire isn't going to take a first-generation computer that's handed down year after year just because you have a five-year refresh cycle. If they need a newer computer to do their job, they'll simply buy one and start using it.*
>
> *We're also seeing a broad shift away from the notion that every device has to be a computer connected somewhere on the network. It's another monumental trend—over the next few years we'll see mobile devices and tablets of every kind in the enterprise.*

The landscape has changed completely, from the mega-app to the micro-app. The people who run the business process now get to make the IT decision.

Wow, think about that for a moment. *The people who run the business process now get to make the IT decision.* That's quite a statement—and for most of us in the IT industry, it really hits home.

Strategic Sourcing and Business Value

For nearly two decades, the idea of outsourcing has been joined at the hip to the idea of cost savings. The narrow focus of the discussion has led to decidedly mixed results. There is no doubt that outsourcing has enabled many companies to achieve truly amazing short-term cost savings. But I would venture a guess that an equal number of companies missed strategic opportunities for long-term growth as they focused their energies relentlessly on cutting costs to the bone.

Rajeev Mehta is chief operating officer, global client services at Cognizant, a worldwide provider of information technology, consulting, and business process outsourcing services. Raj is responsible for all of Cognizant's client-facing activities, and he has a truly unique view of the IT universe. I was happy to catch up with him briefly before the book went to press.

"Obviously, there's been a lot of uncertainty in the past couple of years," says Raj. He sees CIOs in some industries "taking dramatic steps" that will enable their companies to become more nimble, flexible, and competitive.

"The best CIOs are doing a combination of cost-reduction and innovation," says Raj. "They are reducing fixed costs and plowing the savings into innovation. They are spending money more wisely."

Successful CIOs will continue searching for new ways to drive down costs *and* they will focus on achieving strategic business goals. Outsourcing will remain an important part of the equation, says Raj.

This raises an interesting question: Is outsourcing a phenomenon of the down economy, or is it part of the new normal? In some industries, companies are ratcheting up their budgets for technology investment. While they're not exactly going on spending sprees, they are loosening their purse strings. What impact will this additional spending have on their outsourcing strategies?

My guess is that no matter which direction the global economy is heading, outsourcing is here to stay. I think the notion that outsourcing is a passing fad or temporary trend is probably misguided. At the same time, I don't think that CIOs buy into the idea that outsourcing is a goal. Instead they see it as a

> "The best CIOs are doing a combination of cost-reduction and innovation. They are reducing fixed costs and plowing the savings into innovation. They are spending money more wisely."

means to an end, part of an evolving and continuing process of optimization.

To be blunt, outsourcing is now a very real component of the global economy, and most—but not all—CIOs have already baked outsourcing into their IT strategy. CIOs now regard outsourcing as an important element of IT strategy, but not as a strategy unto itself.

Viewed from this perspective, outsourcing can be discussed fairly rationally. Almost all of the CIOs that we interviewed for this chapter basically told us that they had developed much more nuanced perspectives on outsourcing. The "secret" to successful outsourcing is relatively straightforward: You must know in advance what kind of value you are seeking, says Laxman K. Badiga, the CIO of Wipro Technologies. As most of you already know, Wipro is one of the world's largest providers of IT support services. In many respects, companies like Wipro define the outsourcing industry.

"You have to be absolutely clear about the value you expect to receive from an outsourcing arrangement and you have to know how to measure that value," says

Lesson

The "secret" to successful outsourcing is relatively straightforward: You must know in advance what kind of value you are seeking.

Laxman. From a management perspective, that means establishing appropriate metrics and setting up dashboards that will allow the CIO to monitor the performance of the vendor. Dashboards are preferable to reports, because you don't want to find out three months after the fact that something has gone wrong.

So, what does the CIO need to know in order to achieve the level of absolute clarity recommended by Laxman? Here's my short list of what the CIO must know:

- How the business makes money

- How the business interacts with its customers

- How technology can be leveraged to help the business achieve its goals

Of course, you can argue that every effective CIO should already possess this knowledge. I guess that's Laxman's point—you have to approach outsourcing with the same level of understanding and due diligence that you approach every business arrangement. Under no circumstances can you leave it to the vendor to determine if the deal is delivering value—as the CIO, it's *your* responsibility to set the expectations and to verify that they're being met. That's one part of your job that can never be outsourced!

Little Ideas Can Go a Long Way

Although most of us still associate outsourcing with cost-cutting, outsourcing can also be a source of innovation. "You don't always have to look for the big idea," says Laxman. "A lot of little ideas can add up. There's power in incremental innovation."

Smart outsourcing allows the CIO to pursue new ideas without incurring many of the risks. But this is where the concept of taking a more nuanced approach to outsourcing becomes really critical. One of Laxman's standing rules is to look for the right combination of business goal and outsourcer.

What does he mean by this? He is making a simple point that is often overlooked by CIOs: Not all outsourcers are created equal; they all have different strengths and bring different capabilities to the table. Some specialize in providing services, while others specialize in providing new technologies. Some specialize in large-scale engagements, while others specialize in smaller engagements. Some specialize in certain industries. For example, if you're in a highly regulated industry, you might want to think twice about contracting with a vendor that specializes in industries where there is little regulatory oversight.

Lesson

Not all outsourcers are created equal; they all have different strengths and bring different capabilities to the table. Some specialize in providing services, while others specialize in providing new technologies.

My friend Peter Logothetis, the head of technology services at QBE the Americas, offers some great advice on choosing the right vendor: *Be selective.*

"Remember that outsourcing is not a panacea," says Peter. "It's not all or nothing—selective outsourcing has been proven effective over the years. Your vendor partner can make a huge difference, so make sure that you select carefully. Make sure that your expected ROI and SLAs (service level agreements) are crystal clear. Then stay very close to the vendor and take correcting action when necessary."

Resist the urge to settle on a one-size-fits-all solution. Some large vendors offer "one-stop shopping," but chances are that you will be dealing with multiple vendors. Consider it a blessing in disguise—what happens if your "one-stop shopping" vendor decides to change the deal or drops a particular service offering? When I hear about CIOs placing all of their bets with just one or two vendors, I wonder what they're thinking.

Let's Get Granular

In addition to being selective about choosing vendors, you also have to be selective about deciding which pieces of your IT portfolio to outsource. Stephen Davy is the CIO of Newedge Group, a global leader in multiasset brokerage and clearing. Newedge operates in a tightly regulated environment, offering complex services relying on highly sophisticated technologies. Speed, accuracy, and great customer

> "If someone else can do something better
> than we can do it, we'll try to outsource it."

service are essential to the company's success, and Stephen is responsible for choosing the right technology solutions and making absolutely certain that they perform.

Stephen's approach to outsourcing is both disciplined and granular. "Instead of defaulting to outsourcing an entire process, we will first look at the key components of the process and determine what we do very well and what can be improved." His way of determining which steps to outsource and which steps to keep in-house is simple: "If someone else can do something better than we can do it, we'll try to outsource it."

Stephen recommends taking a good hard look at your processes, "breaking them apart and determining where the value can be derived through better customer service, cost savings, etc." I admire his discipline and his willingness to dive into the details of a very complicated business.

For example, the company's e-trading platforms are a core part of its business. But the e-trading experience itself is made up of many processes and steps, and not every one of them has to be performed in-house. In fact, some of the steps can be performed by external vendors more quickly and at less cost. That makes the question—*to outsource, or not to outsource*—relatively easy to answer.

> "If we look at a process and determine that it can be done better, faster, and cheaper if we source it externally, then that's the direction we'll take."

"If we look at a process and determine that it can be done better, faster, and cheaper if we source it externally, then that's the direction we'll take," says Stephen. Echoing Peter's advice earlier, he says it's rarely a good idea to approach sourcing as an "all or nothing" scenario. Examine all the options and determine which ones will create the most value for your business. If outsourcing the entire platform does not make sense, then selectively outsource components of your systems, says Stephen.

Don't Chase Low Unit Costs

During the early days of outsourcing—back when it was still a buzzword—many CIOs succumbed to what I'll call "cost myopia." When you have "cost myopia," you only see the savings that are right in front of you, and you can't see the long-range effects of your cost-cutting tactics.

Stephen Gold, the CIO of Avaya, has lived through enough business trends to know that not every penny saved is a penny earned. If you try to save money by focusing solely on lower unit costs, your tactics might succeed—but your strategy can fail.

Since one of the easiest ways to reduce unit costs is by reducing labor costs, it seems like a no-brainer to outsource projects and services to markets where labor costs less. Sometimes these markets are domestic, in which case you are *nearshoring*, and sometimes they are foreign, in which case you are *off-shoring*. In either instance, you are likely to save money and achieve the lower unit costs you were seeking.

But here's where "cost myopia" can undo your success. "It's important to remember that unit cost is just a piece of the equation," says Steve. "The real issue is determining the cost of a finished product. You will find that it's very much like a manufacturing process—there is not a clean, one-to-one correlation between unit costs and the cost of finished products. So the challenge now is minimizing the leakage and getting the most benefit from your labor arbitrage."

There is also the question of value; as many of us have already noticed, lower costs don't necessarily deliver higher value. I pose this question to you: If the quality of your product or service drops to the point where you start losing customers, what have you really accomplished by lowering your labor costs?

This is the point at which the CIO's leadership abilities are really put to the test. Sourcing is a complex strategy with many moving parts. It is not for the faint of heart, and it is rarely just a matter of finding the lowest labor costs. It involves overcoming barriers posed by culture, language, nationality, and distance.

> ## Lesson
>
> Sourcing is a complex strategy with many moving parts. It is not for the faint of heart, and it is rarely just a matter of finding the lowest labor costs. It involves overcoming barriers posed by culture, language, nationality, and distance.

If the CIO realizes or suspects that a sourcing arrangement isn't working, whether it's outsourcing, in-sourcing, off-shoring or near-shoring, he or she has an obligation to sound the alarm. Now it's no longer a test of leadership—it's a test of character.

A Dose of Common Sense

It's hard to be the CIO, even in the best of times. In difficult times, when everything around you is changing and transformational leadership is required, the job can seem overwhelming. That's why I want to close the book with some practical advice from three CIOs whom I respect greatly.

My good friend Joseph A. Puglisi is the CIO at EMCOR Group, a mechanical and electrical construction and facilities services company with about $5.6 billion in annual revenues. His advice on outsourcing is short and sweet:

The goal is getting the most out of your human capital resources. What is truly unique or adds value to the business, keep in-house. You can outsource all the rest. This is not a terribly radical philosophy, but it works.

Someone with knowledge of the business is always likely to be useful, says Joe. But does it make sense to have someone on staff just to write service tickets or reset passwords?

> *Keep the special skills in-house: business analytics, business intelligence. You need those people to help you understand how well the business is performing . . . and they can add real value to the organization. Look for people with expertise in the business you are supporting.*

Joe also likes to note that only two industries refer to their customers as "users." Sadly, IT is one of them.

Another good friend, Hank Zupnick, is the CIO of GE Real Estate, a unit of GE Capital. From Hank's point of view, neither outsourcing nor the cloud can hold a candle to good IT governance. Given Hank's longevity and success, it's hard to argue with him. Here's his take on governance:

> *IT governance is more than just IT—it's now a critical part of how we're doing business, because it gets the business to think about critical resource allocation and strategic planning issues. It enables us to put IT resources where they're needed the most to help the business.*
>
> *In the past, IT operated in silos. Now we take a more holistic approach. We can look at how spending in one area impacts another area. IT governance brings the entire business leadership management team into the same conversation . . . they can see how IT investments affect the whole business.*

Hank also raised an interesting point about the cloud: If you're already a large global organization, what does the cloud offer in terms of economies of scale? It's a good question, and worth debating.

The Last Word

It's been fun researching and writing this book. It gave me a chance to spend quality time with many old friends, and afforded me opportunities to make new friends. I learned a lot, and now I can hardly wait to start the next book!

By fate or luck, Stuart McGuigan was the last person that we interviewed for this book. Stuart is the CIO of CVS Caremark, the largest pharmacy health care provider in the United States. Like Joe and Hank, he's been around for a while—and he knows the value of patience. Some trends are the heralds of lasting change, others are overshadowed by the "next big thing." My own personal opinion is that the cloud represents a genuine evolutionary step in computing. What impact the cloud will have on business over the next five to ten years is more difficult to say.

When Stuart looks at the cloud, he analyzes it from the CIO's perspective. Here's what he says:

> *There are two groups of CIOs, and it depends on what kind of company you work for. If you are an internal-facing CIO and your job is providing better, faster, cheaper business processes for your company, then the cloud has strategic value for you because it will fundamentally change your cost structure.*
>
> *On the other hand, if you are an external-facing CIO, if the IT system is part of what your company sells to its customers*

and if you have direct contact with the company's customers, then you're not likely to see the cloud as transformational. If IT is part of your competitive advantage in the market, if it's part of a unique product you're selling, then the cloud isn't going to help in a strategic way.

That's some pretty straightforward advice from a guy who knows the drill. The net takeaway is that if it's strategic, you should hang on to it; don't outsource it to the cloud or to anywhere else. If it's not strategic, then go for the cloud—the sky's the limit.

But Stuart didn't leave it there. He wanted me—and you—to understand that being a transformational CIO isn't about mastering the newest technologies or following the latest trends.

It's important for the CIO to be aware of every major technology development. That's one of the exciting things about the job—you have to be conversant with all of the significant new technologies in order to have credibility within the IT department and with your business partners. The depth and breadth of your technical acumen really has to be there.

But to really differentiate yourself as a CIO, to really drive transformation, you need to have a broad understanding of your business . . . you need more depth than the job called for 10 years ago. Today, you need to be part of the C-level team that creates and drives strategy, vision, and priorities across the company.

The way to achieve real transformation is to understand not just how your business operates today, but where it's going tomorrow and where it will be three years from now.

> "The way to achieve real transformation is to understand not just how your business operates today, but where it's going tomorrow and where it will be three years from now."

I can't imagine how to improve on Stuart's words. Plenty of challenges remain. It's hard to predict when the global economy will settle down. A period of calm would be nice, but don't count on it.

One thing is certain. IT will be more important than ever before, and everyone will be looking to the CIO for answers and solutions. I hope that you've picked up some useful information and ideas from the CIOs you've had a chance to "meet" in the pages of this book. You can meet a lot of the people you've just been reading about at the events produced by HMG Strategy. Please visit www.hmgstrategy.com for a full schedule of thought leadership events and executive round-tables. I personally look forward to meeting you, and to hearing your stories.

As IT leaders, we've finally got our seat at the executive table. Now we need to start leading the conversation.

RECOMMENDED READING

Barlow, Mike, and Michael Minelli. *Partnering with the CIO: The Future of IT Sales Seen through the Eyes of Key Decision Makers.* Hoboken, NJ: John Wiley & Sons, 2008.

Benioff, Marc. *Behind the Cloud: The Untold Story of How Salesforce.com Went from Idea to Billion-Dollar Company and Revolutionized an Industry.* San Francisco: Jossey-Bass, 2009.

Broadbent, Marianne, and Ellen S. Kitzis. *The New CIO Leader: Setting the Agenda and Delivering Results.* Boston: Harvard Business School Press, 2005.

Collins, Jim. *Good to Great: Why Some Companies Make the Leap . . . and Others Don't.* New York: HarperBusiness, 2001.

Covey, Stephen R. *The 7 Habits of Highly Effective People: Powerful Lessons in Personal Change.* New York: Free Press, 1989.

Deming, W. Edwards. *The New Economics: For Industry, Government, Education.* Cambridge, MA: MIT Center for Advanced Educational Services, 1994.

Eiras, José Carlos. *The Practical CIO: A Common Sense Guide for Successful IT Leadership.* Hoboken, NJ: John Wiley & Sons, 2010.

Friedman, Thomas L. *The World Is Flat: A Brief History of the 21st Century.* New York: Picador/Farrar, Straus and Giroux, 2005.

Greenleaf, Robert K. *Servant Leadership: A Journey into the Nature of Legitimate Power & Greatness.* New York: Paulist Press, 2002.

Hammer, Michael. *Beyond Reengineering: How the Process-Centered Organization Is Changing Our Work and Our Lives.* New York: HarperBusiness, 1996.

High, Peter A. *World Class IT: Why Businesses Succeed when IT Triumphs.* San Francisco: Jossey-Bass, 2009.

Juran, J. M. *Juran on Quality by Design: The New Steps for Planning Quality into Goods and Services.* New York: Free Press, 1992.

Katzenbach, Jon R. and Douglas K. Smith. *The Wisdom of Teams: Creating the High-Performance Organization.* Boston: Harvard Business School Press, 1993.

Kidder, Tracy. *The Soul of a New Machine.* New York: Little, Brown and Company, 1981.

Kiechel, Walter. *The Lords of Strategy: The Secret Intellectual History of the New Corporate World.* Boston: Harvard Business School Press, 2010.

Kim, W. Chan, and Renee Mauborgne. *Blue Ocean Strategy: How to Create Uncontested Market Space and Make the Competition Irrelevant.* Boston: Harvard Business School Press, 2005.

Kotter, John P. *John P. Kotter on What Leaders Really Do.* Boston: Harvard Business School Press, 1999.

Li, Charlene. *Open Leadership: How Social Technology Can Transform the Way You Lead.* San Francisco: Jossey-Bass, 2010.

Lutchen, Mark D. *Managing IT as a Business: A Survival Guide for CEOs.* Hoboken, NJ: John Wiley & Sons, 2004.

May, Matthew E. *The Elegant Solution: Toyota's Formula for Master Innovation.* New York: Free Press, 2007.

Mirchandani, Vinnie. *The New Polymath: Profiles in Compound-Technology Innovations.* Hoboken, NJ: John Wiley & Sons, 2010.

Rosenberg, Scott. *Dreaming in Code.* New York: Crown Publishers, 2007.

Smith, Gregory S. *Straight to the Top: Becoming a World-Class CIO.* Hoboken, NJ: John Wiley & Sons, 2006.

Watkins, Michael. *The First 90 Days: Critical Strategies for New Leaders at All Levels.* Boston: Harvard Business School Press, 2003.

Zweifel, Thomas D. *Culture Clash: Managing the Global High-Performance Team.* New York: Select Books, 2003.

ABOUT THE AUTHOR

Hunter Muller is president and CEO of HMG Strategy LLC, a global IT strategy consulting firm based in Westport, Connecticut. Mr. Muller has more than 20 years of experience in business strategy consulting. His primary focus is IT organization development, leadership, and business alignment. His concepts and programs have been used successfully by premier corporations worldwide to improve executive performance, enhance collaboration, elevate the role of IT and align enterprise strategy across the topmost levels of management. He lives in Fairfield, Connecticut, with his wife and their two children.

ABOUT HMG STRATEGY, LLC

HMG Strategy, LLC is the leading provider of innovative IT leadership, management and technology support to CIO/ Senior IT executives by focusing on the 360-degree needs of the CIO/IT Leader. The firm's events and services raise thought leadership, knowledge sharing, and networking to the highest level. HMG Strategy provides access to an international network of more than 8,000 global CIO/Senior IT executives, industry experts, and world-class thought leaders.

The firm's *CIO Executive Leadership Series* offers a unique event experience to build relationships with peers and gain the latest insights and best practices for driving increased business value through the use of information technology. Additionally, the firm's partnerships with the world's leading search firms provide CIOs and IT leaders with invaluable insights into the changing role of the technology executive.

For more information, please visit our web site at www .hmgstrategy.com.

INDEX

229